# THE ROAD I KNOW

# THE ROAD I KNOW

by

## STEWART EDWARD WHITE

"I've got a formula I've worked out. I relax my body—rock it in my cradle of confidence—then keep just a shred of attention to see that it doesn't follow me. And then I sneak out onto the road I know. *THE ROAD I KNOW*—that's its name."—BETTY

www.whitecrowbooks.com

# CONTENTS

# INTRODUCTION

The history of this book is in itself an interesting and amusing narrative. After the publication of *The Unobstructed Universe*, Betty informed us that some time must elapse before she would be ready to give another "divulgence." So it occurred to me to examine once again the records of the work Betty did while she was still here. Twice already they had been combed for material—the extracts used in making *The Betty Book* and *Across The Unknown*. While those two books dealt to a large degree with Betty's training, the effort had been to select material from a viewpoint of universal application. Now another viewpoint might prove valuable—that of Betty's own education irrespective of any concern with others than herself.

Perhaps it was largely for my own satisfaction; in any case I did again go through the roughly million and a quarter words that were the records of Betty's work while here. Passages directed at her personally, and no one else, I red-penciled. Next I cut them out and pasted them seriatim.

They totaled nearly two hundred thousand words. For the first time I read them consecutively; and realized that, even with no further arrangement, I had a *narrative*. Furthermore, it had growth-interest, it moved, it climaxed—most gloriously, I thought. Here was obviously a book to be written. Therefore, as I am a writer of books, I set blithely about it.

No light job, I realized. I must tell the story as clearly and simply as possible; I must be accurate, for this sort of thing depends on its integrity; I must use, of those two hundred thousand words, only about one-fifth, lest the reader be confused as well as bored by the repetition necessary for the perfection of Betty's instruction.

My first attempt was to follow chronology and to quote from the records verbatim such excerpts as would best illustrate each step of Betty's progress; with, of course, the necessary editorial connective tissue.

That did not work at all. Betty's instruction was indeed from simple to complex. But definitely it was not chronological. Her orderly graduation from grade to grade was an illusion. My re-perusal of the record made clear to me that actually, in essence, she was given the whole thing at once. I can go back now and perceive that the whole plan and the whole accomplishment is laid out in the first hundred or so pages. In other words, Betty was exposed to the entire experience and instruction much as a photographic film is exposed-sharply to the dot of the opening and closing of the shutter. But, just as the image resulting is latent and must be developed out, so was Betty's comprehension and control latent, and it too must be developed out. Her training was just that.

When once I had got that through my head, the reason for a number of things became clear to me. As, for instance, the Invisibles' maddening habit of abandoning one subject for another, and yet another; returning to each, apparently at random, and certainly at odd times. Now I was able to see that what my logical mind had wanted to be a building process, one brick on another, was in fact the aforesaid developing—out, the whole image becoming more and more defined only as the development proceeded. Whatever might be the illusion of a step-by-step-graded-school; I now saw, as I struggled to work out a chronological presentation of the material, it came about because the Invisibles had successively brought to major prominence, one after the other, single details of the whole image, subduing temporarily all the rest. But never was a detail so clarified as to obviate their need for back-tracking. They were inveterate moppers-up.

Realization that chronology offered no satisfactory frame for this story cleared my mind for a re-write. To do this re-write I had to use a card-index system and from it take all that had been said on any particular phase, whenever and wherever, and then piece it together into a cohering pattern. I had already found that method necessary in making *The Betty Book*, but as the latter dealt only with beginnings, and as this book dealt with the whole picture, I assumed it to be outmoded. So I did it in that sequence. For example, in dealing with some fundamental concept, such as Contact with the Source, I might find it made prominent from, say, about page 1200 to about 1300, but already on page 4 something had been said so apposite that it must be fitted into the later, more extended discussion. And that did not work either. If I quoted a passage entire, it was too long. Worse yet, the new sequence could not be made to behave any more than had the chronological method, because it, too, skipped about. My brother Harwood did grand work in searching records, correlating them, showing their connection. I did a lot of writing. At last we produced something—not the right something. None the less we agreed to be satisfied. And then, as I was ready to pass the manuscript on to the publishers, Betty herself, through Joan, of *The Unobstructed Universe*, turned it down flat. It must be done over again.

"You have," said Betty, reinforced by her coadjutors—I here adopt their own bold habit of putting a condensation, though an accurate one, in quotes—"collected an admirable lot of building blocks. Good building blocks. Your trouble is that you are trying to use them undressed for the job, and even yet you are influenced by the chronological order of their delivery." Now I will begin to quote the Invisibles verbatim. "You see, Betty was *drilled, drilled, drilled* for twenty years, over and over again in the same things, with enormous elaboration in her instruction.

Of COURSE there were many repeats, and in many places. You cannot take your readers in three hours over the whole of those twenty years. Your job is a selective job. You have the obligation to dip into any portion for clarity. You must pick out the bits that seem the sharpest illustration of Betty's systematic travel of the Road—no matter where they come. The public has to have a straight line. It just can't be expected to jump over twenty years.

That helped.

"Furthermore," the Invisibles pointed out, "you are not now writing a didactic book, like *The Betty Book* and *Across The Unknown*. This is a drama, and must be written as such; with three Acts. Act I: How Betty was taught to tap the Source. Act II: Her actual experience after she had learned to do so. Act III: What she did with it, and what it did to her. Only don't present the narrative as three Acts or three Parts; obliterate the joints.

"Now," they further instructed, "use what you have already written as building blocks. Distribute them in three piles, as they fall under one or the other of the three Acts. Then go ahead. And slash out all but the best that applies." This was the scheme of my final rewrite. I had this advantage: I was in weekly touch through Joan, and so could submit my results. Betty and her Invisibles did a lot of "rejiggering," as they called it; recasting, transferring, changing phraseology. So sometimes there may be found a slight variance in my quotation and the original record, or a difference in sequence. And of course it has been necessary for the sake of both clarity and case to condense as of one continuous session the material scattered over several.

But Betty was right in her insistence on the dramatic form. The actual process of her development is in no sense altered by it; rather it becomes clearer, and more easily to be followed.

So this book, like the others, is a collaboration. My brother Harwood and I for the spade work; Darby and Joan for criticisms and suggestions; and Betty and her Invisibles through Joan for personal supervision and approval of the final form.

# CHAPTER 1

# BETTY

## 1.

I must write this book for three reasons: First, to satisfy numerous readers of *The Unobstructed Universe*—the third of the so-called "Betty books" and dictated by her through another psychic after her death—who demand insistently to know "how Betty got that way"; second, to answer questions from the many who, in one way or another, are setting out on the path Betty followed; third, because in her own training Betty was given a pattern for living which could well be used by all of us.

For one by-product of *The Betty Book*, and *Across The Unknown*, written before Betty's death, as well as *The Unobstructed Universe*, published just eighteen months after she died, is a widespread interest in Betty herself. This is more than a mere curiosity as to personality. The latter is well enough defined by what these books report of her words and thoughts. Rather, people want to know—to judge by their letters—how that personality came about. Flow much was her original self? How much was of her own volitional development How much was due to her training by the Invisibles?[1] What was that training? As applied to her, alone, or to be aspired to by others? For of course a good deal of

---

[1] Betty's name for discarnate personalities.

the teachings in the three books is an account of training methods for mankind in general. In a word what hundreds of my correspondents say they want is a biography of Betty.

But not a biography in ordinary definition. Rather a biography of inner life and development. What made her what her three books show her to be? After all, that is the essential aim of any biography—to evaluate the expansion of a person's life, and to examine the influences and happenings and accomplishments that brought this person to wherever he or she had landed by that pausing-time we call death.

# 2.

As with most lives that grow to an ultimate fullness, material in Betty's case is embarrassingly abundant. The difficulty is not of search, but of selection and arrangement. The whole record of the work Betty did in the higher consciousness, both while she was still here and after her death, runs to two thousand four hundred single-spaced pages.

From the two thousand done in her lifetime I have clipped those passages that carried individual instruction. These make over three hundred pages—all material from which to select. Besides, there are, of course, my own recollections of nearly forty years. And in addition, more than a year after her death, I came upon a filing folder containing a miscellany of papers in which from time to time she herself had set down jottings of her own attitude toward the work she was doing, and the impression she had of it.

So, in order to make a start, it is necessary to adopt a point of view.

It must be this: that here is an account of one person's psychic training for a specific job of what later, after her death, she was to call "divulgence" It is quite aside from the purposes—and also the possibilities—to do a portrait or a "character sketch" of Betty. She was as many sided as she was femininely elusive. When I think of attempting it, I share her own impatience with words.

"It's like trying to look at the stars in the daytime," she once complained. "It's perfectly clear until I bring it into the daylight of words, and then it's gone. I don't want to be silly; but the words make one laugh: they are so long-drawn-out for the amount of idea in them. It is as impossible to put my world[2] into words as it is to put the ocean in a

---

[2] Referring to the beyond-earth consciousness into which she had the ability psychically to enter.

bucket." Again and again I remember her interrupting her reporting to express that despair over the impossibility of containing such things in language. Nearing the end of her long experience she wrote this, in her own person, one of the fragments I found in her files.

"Seeing the thing makes it too big for words; they stumble. A condensation of words is a flat crystallized process. Reality is a rounded thing, that pulses. It overflows the mold of words. I cannot tell what my words are doing. I can only radiate myself. That is my form of expression. Take it from me as I pass: it is yours." This gives me a glimpse for my point of view. Betty did radiate herself.

For example, many people, seeing her objectively, remarked on how naturally and without effort she assumed the age of her companions of the moment. She could join children or old people—or anybody between—and BECOME for the time being actually one of them. And obviously this was by no taking thought of condescension or adjustment. She entered their world so interestedly and wholly that she blended with it.

A friend had two children aged six and four. In due time the mother presented them with a baby sister; and the happy idea occurred to her that Peter and Sally could pick out the infant's godmother. They consulted.

"Can we have anyone we want? Anyone at all?" they asked.

"Anyone," the mother assured them, wondering which of a very large family of aunts and cousins it would be.

"Then we'll take Betty White," said they.

Partly because of this faculty, people flocked to Betty with their problems and troubles. She gave them tea—and radiated; and sympathized with them in HER way, which was not at all a coddling way, but as bracing as a frosty morning. She seemed almost to avoid feeding them specific advice; and they went away a little puzzled over why they felt so much better about things. Not that she had no specific advice, when it was really appropriate. Nor that she lacked the moral courage to speak out in meeting when—rarely—an almost brutal bluntness would really do some good.

Three days after she had died a man took me aside.

"I want to tell you something," said he. "Do you remember, a number of years ago, how intolerant I was of people? About little things, I mean?" "I certainly do," I agreed.

"And perhaps you noticed that all at once I quit?" "I certainly did," said I. "Everybody did." "Well, one evening, after I'd been holding forth about so-and-so's lipstick, and what's-her-name's swank and a lot of my usual guff, Betty took me off in a corner. 'See here, Jim!' said she—and I'll never forget how she looked me in the eye—'you are just about the poorest sportsman I know.' " He chuckled ruefully. "That put me back on my heels," said he.

I could well imagine it, for Jim in his day had been a fine amateur athlete, and in sports had always held—and still holds— to the high code of the sportsman. "I swallowed hard and asked her what she meant," continued Jim. " 'I'll tell you,' said she. 'You like to put people into classifications, and then you get mad at them when they do the perfectly natural things that prove you were right!' "That," said Jim, "opened my eyes. Do you know," he went on somewhat hesitatingly, "there had always been a word that somehow I had never found the meaning for. I knew what the dictionary said, and how people used it, and all that, of course; but what I mean is it didn't hold a satisfying idea somehow. Didn't click—" he floundered.

"I get you," said I. I use 'em in my business-words." "Yeah. And then I knew Betty, and when I saw her sitting so small and straight at the head of her table and the little proud poise of her head, and her gaiety and wit, and saw her so gracious to all sorts of people, always, everywhere—no, gracious means condescending somehow, it wasn't that— Well, I got the meaning of my word." "What was the word?" I asked.

"Aristocrat," said Jim.

I remember Austin Strong sitting silent at a gay dinner party, his elbow on the table, his chin in his hand, watching Betty with the playwright's look of speculation and analysis, and finally giving it up with a sigh.

"That damned charm! " he muttered, shaking his head.

For Betty's outer person was just that. Charm—charm and gaiety. And a delightful wit, that was wit because of new angles of view, and of modes of expression so original and unexpected that the stiffest formalist must yield to it. I suppose it carried so far because it was in no way artificial, or considered, or thought over. It was Betty's normal language, the way she thought, and therefore the way she spoke. Like all wit of that kind, while unforgettable, it is equally unquotable. In report most of it becomes mere museum mountings without the breath of life. But no one was ever bored with Betty. Even though what she had to say might be dryly statistical, one found himself alert for what she would make of it. I lived with her thirty-five years, and—though there was plenty more—in all that time I was always relishingly entertained, and continually anticipating what next.

4

However, it was not the outer expression but the inner person that made the charm memorable; made it stick, as it were. Apparently people never forgot Betty. She made an indelible impress. After her death I received several hundred letters—and I mean *letters* pages long, not mere "notes of condolence." An extraordinary number of them were from people who had met her JUST ONCE and years before—from twelve to thirty-two years before—but who wrote as though her personality were to them as of yesterday. On my return home, after her death in Upland in 1939, my secretary told me that a very aged Negro had hobbled in to say how sorry he was. "Mis' White, she was FOLKS," said he. Investigating, I found that this man had given the windows of our new house their first washing when the builders had cleared out, and that was all the contact he had ever had with us. The house was finished in 1919.

Now I am not setting down these things as a partisan of Betty. I am her partisan of course; but my point is that so became and so remained everyone who had even casual contact with her. And, I am convinced, this has been true, not essentially because of the outer characteristics, but because of what she called "radiation." This power of radiation probably was inborn; the training of her Invisibles was directed toward its conscious unfoldment. I say it must have been inborn, for obviously there must have been something to work on, something to develop. So, though this biography is of the inner, it must be built on a foundation of outer circumstance, and we must deal briefly with the latter.

Betty was a little woman. She always firmly maintained that five feet was her "official height." For thirty years I made her a standing offer of five hundred dollars— for herself or her pet charity— if measurement would prove that claim; and a further offer of one hundred dollars if she would be measured at all! These offers she always refused with dignity. Nevertheless her proportions were so harmonious, and she carried herself with so spirited a lift of the head that her tiny stature had its own unique personality. People called her "exquisite"; I suppose that was the adjective most often used to describe her. Also she seemed to have the secret of perpetual youth. Until her last illness at fifty-nine, her figure was as slender and well-formed; her hair as soft and abundant and brown—she never had a gray hair; her skin as smooth; her cheeks as shell pink as at twenty-five. This is not my own—and fatuous opinion, but the occasion for wondering remark by so many of her friends that I have to believe it factually true.

"Why!" exclaimed a visitor, seeing her in bed with her hair about her on the pillow, "she's just like a little girl!" The statement of all this would have slight importance, were it not for the possibility—worth considering—that this too may well be the "outward and visible sign" of that inner thing she called RADIATION—her development of which we are to deal with in this book.

Continuing for the moment with the physical, Betty's small body was soft and feminine, but somewhere in it—or in the spirit that animated it—dwelt a deceptive endurance. Before my marriage I had led a rather unusually venturesome life, in all parts of the world, and this I continued afterward. And Betty went along. Horse and pack in the Sierra and Rockies; the cattle roundups of Arizona; afoot and back-packing in the tailless back country; canoe travel; fourteen months of safari in Central Africa; years of cruising along the Pacific Northwest coast. Nor was she taken along as a considered and pampered sightseer. Naturally I eased things for her when I could, but often it was not possible to ease things at all. These were no play trips. The mountain travel was before the days of made trails and guides: we carried everything we needed—even to horseshoes—on horseback, for five months at a time; we slept without cots or tents; and sometimes rode fourteen hours of a day, and then cooked and made camp. Arizona of those days had no dude ranches: Betty slept on the ground, and arose at four to a real cow-puncher breakfast of thin, greasy fried steak and soggy soda biscuits, and saw no more food until nightfall; and in the hours between rode the breakneck lava doing her full share in the cattle drive. On foot trips in the woods she carried her own appropriate back-pack. The safari of her day in Africa was no modern Cook's tour of prearrangement: we took our bearers from the savage tribes. As for Alaska—well, one day she went out on a shore excursion with Charley, who is six feet one and weighs a hard hundred and eighty pounds.

Charley promised to take good care of her. On their return he flopped into a deck chair.

"If ever," he cried fervently, "you get me out in the woods again with that—with that dam little chipmunk— " I remember at the White House seeing Theodore Roosevelt staring across the lunch table at her small and vivacious personality decked in the pink things and ostrich-feathered big hat of the period. "I don't believe it," he muttered to me at last.

Her steady coolness and courage were probably also manifestations of an inner quality. In strenuous outdoor life there must be emergencies. She met them. If the nature of the show was one—a lion muss-up for instance—to which she could not contribute, she was behind the guns, where she belonged, and keeping quiet. When there was something she could do, she did it, calmly and efficiently. Sometimes that something took cool headedness, sometimes real courage. Once in Africa a buffalo appeared, silently, unexpectedly, actually to crop the top of a low bush beneath which she was sitting. The instinctive feminine reaction—and the usual masculine, I suspect—would be to squawk and flutter, and so to be instantly crushed by hoof and horn. Betty slowly eased herself flat to the ground and lay immobile the eternity before I could get hold of a rifle. Of a wild and stormy day that kept me close to an ailing and uncertain engine of the little cruiser she and I conducted for some years up the British Columbia coast, a violent sea threw her against the spokes of the wheel where she stood at her post, breaking two of her ribs. I did not know this until we reached a port, three days later.

"Why should I tell you?" she answered my reproach. "There was nothing to be done about it." Suffering of others tore her heart; but she could cut steadily and coolly into human flesh, when a backwood's accident made minor surgery necessary. I've seen her cut a deeply imbedded fishhook from a man's arm with entire coolness and dexterity, a lot calmer than the man himself until afterward! Then she wailed.

A curious and interesting angle to this is that she came to it not only without preparatory training or experience, but with what ordinarily would be called a handicap. She was raised in Newport, with subsequent backgrounds of fashionable hotels in Bermuda, Florida, Jamaica, California. From babyhood to the very noon I married her she was tagged about by a personal Negro "mammy," who dressed and undressed her, and picked up things after her. Her education was in an "exclusive" girls' school, where, she later confessed, she learned "the whole of nothing."

So, for a honeymoon, I took her into the Sierra where she slept on the ground and no tent; ate camp food of my cooking; and got along by way of wardrobe—for four months—on what she could stuff into one small duffle bag. This seemed to me then a nice easy trip! I had been up in the Hudson Bay region, carrying everything I owned on my back; and here we had horses to do the carrying, and I did the cooking and hard work, and all Betty had to do was sit a horse and look at the scenery—and—oh, yes—make the bed and help pack and do the laundry and maybe wash dishes occasionally when the horses strayed! Taking a lot for granted in the beginning, only years later did I realize that I was favored with a very miracle of adaptability. For Betty had a good time always; a joyous, zestful, outflinging good time. She always had that, right through life.

For her the world was, indeed, full of a number of things. She scorned the thought that it could ever be otherwise. "Old age?" she answered someone's pessimistic objection. "But why old age at all? Old age is when you stop looking at things!" Sometimes, to tease her, I would describe her as the world's greatest mongrel, and to prove it I would gabble, almost in a breath, as it were, the catalogue of her mixture.

"She is half-Spanish, half-Scotch. She was born on the Isthmus of Panama, raised in Newport, and married a Westerner. Her mother was a Roman Catholic, her father a Scotch Presbyterian, she was brought up an Episcopalian, and now what is she?" And this, together with my suggestion that she was less than five feet tall, she ignored with dignity.

One gift, that she had always possessed, was greatly developed, or perhaps only more clearly disclosed, by the life she led with me. That was her kinship with animals as well as with human beings. She understood them, and—more important—they understood and had confidence in her. Often I have rounded the bend of an Alaskan river to see Betty, sitting on a cut bank, talking to a raven beside her. On my appearance the bird would at once fly away—though I was, perhaps, a hundred yards distant, and Betty but two or three feet. We were having a good deal to do, at that time, with the big Alaska brown—sometimes called Kodiak-bear, and as we were taking moving pictures and not killing, the camera demanded much shorter range than the rifle. While these animals by no means deserve their reputation for ferocity, they are to be treated with respect. One day Betty, walking upstream, met one of them, somewhere between twelve and fifteen hundred pounds of live bear, walking down stream. She stopped, drew herself up to her full five feet (?), and pointed a commanding finger.

"Now you are a nice bear," said she, "but you go away! Go away!" she repeated more sharply.

The bear stopped, looked at her to see if she meant it, dropped his ears exactly as a well-mannered dog obeys, and turned off at right angles into the brush.

After a few such experiences—not only with bear, but with deer and other wild creatures—I began to pass up the movie when occasionally she would say: "I wouldn't fool with that one, he's cross." Quite often, when we had anchored near shore, a yellow jacket would visit the cabin. Betty would hold her hands about a foot apart and extended toward the insect, and—believe it or not—that creature would go out of the hatch and away like a bullet.

"I just convey to him that this is not a nice place for a yellow jacket to be," she answered our queries. But she confessed she could do nothing with flies.

"They are too scatter-minded," she explained.

When we married I owned a horse named Bullet. Bullet was a wonderful mountain horse, but he demanded respect. Even I, whom he knew well, had to get aboard with neatness and dispatch. Bullet tolerated no sloppiness. If I fumbled or dawdled, or caught against the cantle, or anything like that, down went his head in protest and up arched his back. But he was not treacherous. Once I was properly in the saddle, I could do anything the lawful occasions of rough mountain travel demanded, even to picking things off the ground or dismounting, mounting on the wrong side, or waving slickers to head pack animals, or shooting a gun—anything; anything at all. That was for me. But he was not so tolerant of others. Indeed, I did not permit others to ride him after a friend of mine—a fine rider—found himself on one side of a high sharp picket fence and Bullet on the other, when the dust had cleared. That is, I permitted no others but Betty. She could not reach both the pommel and the stirrup from the ground, so she wound the saddle strings around her hand and literally shinned up Bullet's foreleg, and Bullet turned his head to watch benignly, standing like a rock until she was well settled in the saddle, his ears on the half-slant of virtue.

My picket-fence friend was horrified when he first saw this performance.

"It's criminal!" he expostulated vehemently. "Some day he'll kill her." But I knew better, and so did Betty. And so did Bullet.

Anecdote of this sort I could recall by the score. But one other picture seems to insist.

One day the Austin Strongs, Betty and I were wandering through San Francisco's open-air zoo. Betty was some distance ahead of us. We saw her stop for a long time before a cage in which dozed a great lion, broadly oblivious to the throngs of people passing or trying vainly to attract his attention. After a time Betty walked away. That lion opened his eyes, got to his feet, followed to the end of the cage, lifted his head staring after the tiny figure just as far as he could see her in the crowd. Then he sighed, lay down again, and closed his eyes.

We pursued Betty.

"What were you doing to that lion? " we demanded.

"I made him pictures," said she simply, "pictures of the African veldt." I shall get no further piling up such incidents. After all it is not really a portrait that is intended, but only to show a training in spirituality. Granted that spirituality is, as Betty expresses it, such a "skiddy" word, its avowed practitioner is ordinarily looked upon as someone apart from hearty living. I have sought to suggest that Betty was in no sense apart—apart from anything She had a healthy and holy horror of anything resembling asceticism. She used and enjoyed to the full all of human life. "Asceticism means you are afraid of something," she pointed out. She had an equal horror of any taint of superiority, of the "teacher" attitude.

Zest; joyousness; the glow of radiation; a genuine love "for all things great and small." Simple elements of personality, but rarely to be met unalloyed. People felt the rarity, without recognizing it.

One day, months after Betty's death, I was driving home from the city, with a friend—a business man.

"Wasn't it wonderful," he said out of a prolonged silence, "that they loaned us Betty for a little while."

# CHAPTER 2

# EVERYBODY IS PSYCHIC

## 1.

There may have been, in the world's history, others who have been as rigorously and systematically trained as was Betty for her especial job of divulgence. If so the details of their training, if recorded, have not come to my attention. The capacity for mediumship is beyond question a natural gift. But, like any other natural gift, it is of itself imperfect, unreliable in detail. Above all, without intelligent cultivation, it does not progress. Used prematurely or excessively it often appears to deteriorate, perhaps finally to atrophy to nothing.

There is close analogy to a natural singing voice that is used too soon or too much. No reasonable teacher allows that. He wants reliability, stability, and progress.

Now Betty had this natural gift of mediumship to a high degree. But until 1919 nobody—not even she or I recognized it technically. Her friends knew her as one with exquisitely delicate human sympathies and relationships, extraordinarily sensitive and responsive to the deeper beauties of life, and possessed of almost uncanny intuitions. Then occurred the small "chance" experience which presently she herself will describe.

She found herself unexpectedly in what is called "psychic" touch with an unseen world.

This is, of course, no very unusual occurrence. Indeed, since I came out openly on the whole subject, I've had so many people write me and recount their own experiences, that I am almost tempted to say it is a rather common occurrence! But most such persons run a standardized course.

As it ordinarily goes, the psychic gets in touch, by one technique or another, with what seems indubitably to be discarnate intelligences.

These latter give "communications." Sometimes these communications are convincing enough to withstand skilled and dispassionate appraisal of genuineness; though even then, more often than not, they show a strong dash of "coloring" from the medium's subconscious. Both the new-fledged medium and the sitters are enormously impressed. They feel that to them is being confided a message of sacred trust. The world must be told of it! Indeed, not infrequently they feel they have been especially instructed to go forth and proclaim. The psychic has said—and the statement has been accepted at face value—"you are chosen" to give forth a revelation. Naturally this sense of almost sacred obligation results in a book or pamphlet, generally privately printed, distributed in all good faith, and with all confidence that it is going to arouse said world. Its failure to do so is a most disheartening and disillusioning puzzle.

It should not be. There are really only two things wrong in the experience, though nine-tenths—perhaps even a larger percentage—of the effort is true and constructive.

One of the two things is the assumption that the "message" is intended for the world. That is natural enough. Indeed, haven't they been so told? It is flattering to be especially "chosen," and what reason, as yet, is there to doubt? But I am sorry to say that long and varied experience has made me leery of just that statement. It occurs too often. I am convinced it indicates either that the whole occurrence is phony, or that the medium's subconscious is at work. Not that the medium is really at fault, or exhibiting undue egotism. The material given is indeed important, if only a recasting of proverbial wisdom; and that importance exaggerates itself in the medium's subconscious. The "message" is real, but it is not addressed to the world; it is addressed to just those few people of that small group, fitting their need for the couching of old truths in language appropriate to their understanding; and is meant only for their own development and unfoldment. They are getting personal attention. It fits them. Also many others in the world are getting personal attention. Very rarely, and only in emergency of world need, is the divulgence intentionally conveyed in such form as to merit widespread acceptance.

That is why such books as Margaret Cameron's *The Seven Purposes*, Lodge's *Raymond*, in spite of all its obvious "coloring," and the anonymous *Our Unseen Guest* commanded a public. An emergency existed.

In Betty's case there seemed to be no such urgency. Quite the contrary, indeed. Nor were we told that we were especially selected, except for our own sakes. And it was nearly eighteen years before we were allowed to think the job was in any way public.

*The Betty Book* did not come out until 1937, and that, I think, was conceded rather to satisfy our own uneasiness over the enormous accumulation of record, than because of any desire on the part of the Invisibles. Before that they had appeased our instinct for order by helping us put together an arrangement of the teaching comprised in the first four hundred pages of records, covering the first year and a half.

This was duplicated in fifteen or twenty mimeographed copies, and had a wide lending circulation among personal friends and acquaintances. It was the basis on which—in 1935 some fifteen years later—we began to build *The Betty Book*. By that time the records had grown to 1993 pages.

Nevertheless, we were held, in *The Betty Book*, to the material of that first year and a half-approximately those first 400 pages. Only a primer was called for, said the Invisibles, hinting—but vaguely—that the more advanced work would be collated and dealt with later. The "primer" was not actually published until 1937.

Encouraged by its reception, my brother and I plunged into selecting from the now bewilderingly abundant material, and emerged with the compilation we called *Across The Unknown*. This dealt with Betty's later experiences. It by no means exhausted the records, but we had more or less caught up to Betty, so to speak, and now we could go on with her in whatever were to be her further explorations. That looked like the job; and a good job it was.

Therefore when Betty fell so desperately ill, in 1938, we had every confidence in her recovery. She had been rigorously and carefully trained for twenty years, and seemed to us just to have arrived at the point of her real effectiveness as a tool: surely that tool must be put to use! It did not make sense otherwise. Nevertheless when she did die, we had no feeling of frustration. The very circumstance of her death appeared to point the climax of truth to the whole episode of tier long training. I wrote of that in the final chapter to *Across The Unknown*. I have quoted from it once before in *The Unobstructed Universe*.

Nevertheless, here, for the third time, it appears in print as necessary background to the whole picture.

"You know," I wrote of my experience immediately following her death,[3] "the cozy, intimate feeling of companionship you get sometimes when you are in the same room; perhaps each reading a book; not speaking, not even looking at one another. It is tenuous, an evanescent thing—one that we too often fail to savor and appreciate. Sometimes, in fact, it takes an evening or two of empty solitude to make us realize how substantial and important it really is.

"Well, within a very few minutes that companionship flooded through my whole being from Betty, but in an intensity and purity of which I had previously had no conception. It was the same thing, but a hundred, a thousand times stronger. And I realized that it more than compensated for the little fact that she had stepped across, because it was the thing that all our physical activities together had striven for, but—compared with this—had gained only dimly and in part. Why not? Actually it was doing perfectly what all these other things had only groped for. So what use the other things? And why should I miss them? "Does this sound fantastic? Maybe; but it is as real and solid as the chair I am sitting on. So much so that I have never in my life been so filled with pure happiness. No despair; no devastation; just a deeper happiness than I have experienced with her ever before, save in the brief moments when everything harmonized in fulfillment.

"This, I now believe, is the 'great blossom' of which the Invisibles spoke: the final significance to which all of Betty's twenty years of work was to lead. Here is her concrete proof of one reward that can come to those who follow in her footsteps, her final evidence that her instrument of twenty years' forging is strong enough to withstand the supreme test.

## 2.

So we imagined the job finished—except perhaps in the further use of material from the records. Then occurred my visit to renew friendship with Darby and Joan, of *Our Unseen Guest*, and through Joan came Betty's "divulgence" of that amazing book, *The Unobstructed Universe*. Soon it was blazingly clear that without Betty's twenty years of training HERE in our obstructed universe such a "divulgence" would

---

[3]  For the whole passage, see Across The Unknown, page 331.

have been totally impossible from her present unobstructed phase of living *there*: that it would be equally impossible for her to have given it from here; that—obscurely to us at first, but evident to us now—all along she and Joan had been developing apart as a team now to work together. That the job had just begun! As an end of effort the previous two books fell into relative unimportance. They had been only indirectly part of the intention.

"They were parts of my training that happened to get published," said Betty, while giving *The Unobstructed Universe*. She did not deny the value so many people found in them: they were—and are—worthwhile.

"But," said she, "they should really be read AFTER this one." Curiously, as it seemed to us at the time, she had never taken much part nor great interest in the writing of the first two books, either on her own, or when she was working in her "other consciousness" with the Invisibles. "These books," she told us—from that other consciousness—"are not intended to reach many people—yet." But of the third book, from the very start, she, now a permanent dweller in the other consciousness, confidently predicted, "this is going to make a stir"; "this is going to be taken up by the scientists." We flatly disbelieved her. Fully as we recognized the novelty and value of the book's contents, we considered it limited in appeal to the small and very specialized public already interested in such things. We were wrong. It sold twelve printings in its first three and a half months; it elicited literally hundreds of letters; it has been preached on from many pulpits. And, as for the scientists, I have dozens of letters, from all varieties of them, some of each sort professing to find in the book revolutionary principles that open to them new fields in their own specialties.

In view of this, and in view of the fact that Betty promises us further "divulgence" in due time, an account of her twenty years of rigorous preparation, seems now to be strongly indicated.

# CHAPTER 3

# BETTY'S OWN NARRATIVE

## 1.

A FEW months ago, and quite by chance, I came across a number of folders in which Betty had filed a mass of papers and notes. Among them were sheets on which she had written down—apparently at irregular intervals—her own personal impressions concerning all this long arduous discipline and unfoldment. They are fragmentary and undated. I think perhaps they were notes for a personal narrative which was never undertaken. They do, however, give an invaluable background for the account of her training drawn from the actual records. The following—as far as it goes—is what Betty herself, in her own normal person, wrote of her thoughts and impressions concerning her experience. It is as she wrote it, except that I have here and there inserted a word obviously intended, or rearranged certain material out of logical order. But in no case have such slight alterations changed the sense.

## 2.

"Most of us," her notes began, "come into contact, sooner or later, with some one who has had experiences of a startling nature, something that points to the existence of powers beyond those we ordinarily possess. If such an experience happens to us personally, it is all the more arresting because we are forced to believe in it and try to explain it.

Few things that can happen to us in the course of life are as thrilling—in the true sense of the word—as staggering, as these glimpses of an extension of our powers. Something long buried in us seems to come to the surface temporarily and convince us that the thing experienced is quite possible and true. I say temporarily, because at first it has tremendous tides. The high tide of our first enthusiasm has an ebb that drains away everything, leaving us far away from the original flooding inspiration. Then everything goes cold, flat and hopelessly inaccessible, if not actually repellent.

"It seems that the development of these higher powers within us runs a definite course, with symptoms almost as recognizable as measles.

Exaltation and security; then flat-tired incapacities of all kinds, and doubt. After suffering long from each symptom, as if it were fatal, I have tried to sum up the whole experience from the vantage point of ten years of constant struggle.

"Why the struggle? I do not know. Certainly neither sorrow nor lack of life's experiences turned me to it. It must be born in people. Perhaps it was a gift from a long line of Scotch ancestors, all of whom seem to have had to struggle thus. At any rate, it has all happened along with an exceptionally busy adventuresome life, and a happily married one.

"To tidy up the subject in my own mind I have hunted up some notes written in the very beginning of my psychic experiences.

"One night during dinner we and a friend discussed a psychic book I had been reading. The friend then told of her success in Russia at moving tables and we were inspired to try it ourselves, solemnly swearing 'on honor' to be honest in the experiment. After dinner the lamps were put out and by the firelight, kneeling around a small table, with tips of fingers touching the top and our little fingers joined, we three sat quietly waiting. After a brief wait we were thrilled by a strange feeling of vitality in the table and movement began. Until midnight we experimented, too spellbound with our own astonishing success to carry out our original engagement to go to the 'movies.' "The table tipped once for yes and twice for no, and moved around the room in designated directions. Next we tried pencil and paper and had a little success. Hearts were repeatedly drawn, 'love' and 'Helen' written, and a few uncertain attempts at words. These were done with a pencil held in one person's hand, with another person's hand placed lightly upon it, the elbows off the table.

"On a subsequent evening some friends came to call, bringing with them a Ouija board. With the usual protective veneer of suppressed hilarity, we proceeded to experiment with this. We tried the board with different combinations of people, receiving a jumble of sense and nonsense, vague advice on business, unremembered anecdotes of childhood playmates. Some of the names spelled out were familiar and others strange. The impression left was one of confusion, but also a certain bewildering credence. The first thing that really moved me was a message from my old colored nurse, an adored foster mother, who was with me from my birth to my marriage. Then came my mother, who had died in my babyhood, and called me daughter, a name strangely novel and beautiful to me as I had never known my parents. She urged me to try writing with a pencil.

"This in private I tried to do, with growing success each day. At first the letters all ran along together and had to be separated into words. I kept my eyes closed in order to free my mind of all outside distractions, but this was not so necessary later except when my attention wandered or became concentrated on the words being written.

The messages were very simple ones urging me to continue, but they brought me a strange and beautiful elation. My mother confirmed my lifelong impression that my family (nearly all of whom had died in my childhood) had been watching over me and trying to influence me for years. I was pathetically almost frantically implored to have patience, faith and persistence in spite of failure or interruptions from opposing forces. Great insistence was made upon practice, constant practice, and keeping my mind a blank.

"'This is only a weak beginning. You will develop rapidly if you will only follow our influence. Will you make a little shrine of yourself for us to work through? There are many of us trying to get at our loved ones. After a while you will be able to talk and act with us. We want you to begin to practice giving yourself up to us so that we can talk through you. It will take some time for you cannot know our laws. Sit quietly a while, think of cosmic things, we will help.' "In the meantime a telegram had come with the sad news that Lizzie, a much loved and devoted friend and retainer of the family, had had a stroke of apoplexy and was unconscious. I asked the Ouija board[4] if she would recover.

---

[4]  But by this time Betty had, I thought, abandoned the Ouija board for automatic writing. This may be a slip on her part, or she may indeed have recurred for this purpose to the earlier method.

"'Do not worry, she will not suffer long, she will come to us in ten days,' the board answered.

"I said, 'Are you sure?' "'About,' was the answer. In twelve days she was dead.

"At about this time, also, came a sudden written message from Stewart's father, asking him to give financial aid to a friend of ours who needed capital to give him a business opportunity.

"'Write a letter at once, now,' the message urged, 'it is a question of time.' "We were at that moment in a friend's camp at some distance from a post office, with no known communication that day, but no sooner was the letter written than a man arrived who was delivering something and returning at once, and to him we entrusted the letter. Later it proved that time was an important element in receiving the information regarding the loan.

"These circumstances, or coincidences, if you prefer, had at least the effect of arousing our interest. We determined to investigate slowly and carefully and honestly each step, not letting ourselves be carried away by any desire of our own to believe or disbelieve.

"Mediumship was now being urged upon me in the messages. My first and second efforts at this caused a strange sensation of being lifted out of myself and almost slipping over the edge, as when just losing consciousness under ether. Before letting me go, however, Stewart demanded assurance that I was really in the hands of my friends and for this purpose asked for a test. His father was asked to give the name of an old lumberman employed years ago, a name unknown to me. A curious jumble of names of old 'lumber jacks' came, all unknown to me, some of them known to Stewart, but the desired name did not come and the test failed.

"The next day this was written. 'It will be impossible for us to answer the tests for the present, because your father is not yet in our sphere and cannot communicate directly; as soon as that is made possible we will be able to convince you. At present it would only confuse you and not add to your faith. It is disappointing to us to have the delay, but we understand and do not blame you. It will be invaluable to have Stewart for us, so we must wait. We will let you know when we are ready for the tests. In the meantime we will write you regularly and try to prepare your mind for what we want you to do. We will not make you nervous. We promise that, and that no evil will come to you, for there are too many of us working over you. That is the great strength and hope of your particular case. It is all for your happiness. Dear child, fear not; tell Stewart to give you up to our care every day for a little while. From earliest times in the history of the race a few have experienced what you are now doing. It is now daily becoming more common, and we hope soon to be acknowledged before the world.

"'Give your mind to thoughts of our love for you and yours for us. It is the stepping stone which brings us safely across. We cannot succeed without that. Love is a powerful medium of communication. So much depends on you, we can only succeed if you do your part.'" All this—the table tipping, Ouija board, the visit to the friend's camp, the death of Lizzie—I recall as having happened in 1919.— S.E.W.

"During this time and subsequently," Betty's notes go on, "my mind was exalted with my secret. I was supremely happy. There followed, however, a sinking, haunting period of lack of faith in myself. All I had ever learned of the subconscious mind tormented me with questionings. Could I be hypnotizing myself with this thing? The beautiful nearness and protection, which had been a lifelong companionship, cherished in the very fiber of me,[5] suddenly fell away, leaving me lonesome as a deserted soul. This temporary loss and struggle, in milder form, took place again and again after receiving various false predictions.

"Several books of similar experiences read about this time, and a wholesome and too lively sense of humor which occasionally brought on a childish and rather hysterically amused attitude towards the whole affair undoubtedly saved me at this period.

"My first experience of this kind of false prediction was astounding. I had asked a very foolish question, 'Will I have a long life?' The answer was, 'You will die of cancer of the stomach in ten months.' Feeling a great personal interest in this statement and that something really should be done about it, I rallied a little efficiency and asked if I should go and have an X ray taken. The answer was rather blighting to a happy psychic, 'No, it will do no good.' "I was not particularly depressed by this, strange as it may seem. My principal impression was that it was really sad for Stewart and that I must certainly hurry and finish up a lot of things at loose ends. It was honestly rather an exciting stimulating thought and if I could only persist in it efficiency would be tremendously increased. At once, however, a less hurried hand wrote, 'You will live many happy years.' "This was my first experience with what I later learned to call the 'Blind Forces.' I had been repeatedly

---

[5]  Betty had always, though vaguely, felt herself under the care of the unseen. S.E.W.

warned to maintain my faith in spite of interruptions from opposing forces, so I was not altogether unprepared. A number of almost childish pranks followed at intervals.

Curiously enough, in some there seemed to be an element of truth, perverted in transmission. For instance, while sitting at a table in a hotel dining room my hand had a feverishly insistent desire to write. I took a menu, and on the back, with a haste which cramped my hand, received this message, 'Your Aunt Nina is in danger. She is in an automobile wreck. It is on the road east of Hollywood (this after a slight hesitation).

Bertha will be injured. You will be called on the telephone to go to them. Do not leave the hotel this afternoon. We did not foresee it.' "Shortly afterwards my Aunt and Bertha rang up and talked to me on the telephone, as hale and hearty as ever. On returning home, however, I found that at the time my butler and his wife had been in an automobile wreck which proved very serious for her, poor girl, as her face was badly scarred for life.

"A rather amusing prediction received in the same hurried manner while on a street car and written on a paper torn from a package, announced that there would be a change in my fortunes; that I was to be left a large sum of money by someone the spirits had advised to leave it to me for their work. Rather a moral lecture followed, telling me to decide what was the most far-reaching benefit I could confer with it, and to act while I was in my prime; and giving me clearly to understand that I was not to use the money for myself in any way; that they would keep a suspicious eye on me. It continued, 'you do not believe, you are not as excited about this as we are. We should like to talk to you more about this wonderful gift, but you seem apathetic,' as indeed I was, for I knew that it was not true. At the end, 'This is not true, Mother,' was written.

"I felt quite resentful and indignant over these things, even though I had been more or less prepared to expect them, or some form of 'interference.' Gradually, however, my faith grew until, even in the midst of my indignation over what seemed a very flagrant case of attempt to deceive me, I still never doubted that an explanation would be given, and my desire to continue was as strong as ever. Only the surface of me demanded that I assume an injured frame of mind, as of a virtuous person badly treated. Always, too, I guarded myself against too easy credulity. The etiquette of my world required certain apologies, but the Supreme Court within me was rather lenient about the whole disgraceful affair. There was no need in being huffy about it for no satisfactory apologies were given, outside of vague remarks about these scapegoat forces every failure is hung on. As for example thus—'the forces which intruded on you yesterday will not be allowed to make an attack upon you again.' I preserved a dignified and judicial silence as there seemed nothing else to do. This promise of better protection was faithfully kept, for on two evenings soon after this, when the writing faltered or became tense, the pencil was forcibly knocked out of my hand. The false messages had always been delivered with feverish haste and great force in contrast to the calm and deliberation of other communications, especially those from my father. This 'cutting-in' haste had the virtue of making me able to recognize instantly and discount anything thus received. The imitation high moral tone adopted in the announcement of my coming fortune was particularly absurd. After the first irritation had passed, it seemed rather humorous to me and I felt as if dealing with children who had dressed up 'to play lady and go calling.'

# 3.

I want to break in on Betty's manuscript at this point to emphasize the strength of the opposing currents against which she persisted. As she says, the communications themselves were sprinkled with inconsistencies and crude falsifications for which, as yet, no sufficing explanations—or apologies were offered. And she had not, of course, yet learned to edit such things out. I should not have been much surprised if she had chucked the whole thing. It took some resolution to set aside, from an exceptionally busy and colorful life, so much time for anything so unreliable and doubtful.

For her life was indeed busy and colorful. California in winter attracts a great variety and number of people from all over the world. Our friends derisively nicknamed our house "The White Hotel" because of the almost continuous occupation of our guest rooms. We gave dinners—many of them and because we invited people in order to know them, we never set table for more than ten. Betty served tea every afternoon, soon attracting her own little circle of the faithful who came as often as they could without shame. And beside the regulars she used that hour to entertain such visitors as she could not quite work in on the "hotel" or a dinner. The flow through our house was almost continuous. We had about everything—writers, soldiers, states-men, ranchmen, cowboys, fishermen, artists, stage people, a Japanese ambassador, a Persian mystic, a Celanese prince. No end to them. A brilliant company on the whole; a congenial company too, made so by Betty's uncanny ability to lift people to their own tops.

The graceful and gracious conduct of this constantly shifting so-cial menagerie would seem a full-time job, but it was actually only one side issue of Betty's many lively interests. She had three acres of garden which she managed with the labor of one man—and it was HER gar-den, not a gardener's garden—minutely diagrammed by her, down to the planting of the last pansy, on huge sheets of wrapping paper. With a truly professional eye she took into account color, height, background, arrangement, the seasons. And the results she achieved brought her literally dozens of blue ribbons in competition with the big estates em-ploying as many as ten gardeners. In this garden also she collected and acclimated rare foreign plants and shrubs—concerning which even yet I am called upon to write very ignorant replies to enquiring scientists.

It was this collection which gained her, in the U. S. Department of Agriculture, the unsought listing as Agricultural Explorer. In addition she was very active in our local Garden Club, injecting into its numerous affairs certain quaint and Betty's conceits of her own. For example, she established (for the Annual Flower Shows) an especial award which was known as the Smell Trophy to be given for that arrangement judged to produce the most pleasing blend of perfume! And another—in cash—to the sculptor submitting the design for a bird fountain, faucet head, or what-not which was at once the most artistic and could be the most cheaply reproduced. All this likewise would seem to be a full-time job.

But she had just as much interest and zest to put into all sorts of other outlets for her insatiable energy. She wove textiles of her own designs; she had a potter's wheel and did some really charming orig-inal pottery; she modeled in clay. She was deeply interested in Ori-ental Art of which she made a serious study. She wrote—for her own satisfaction, since she showed it to nobody—the gayest light verse. I found dozens of such poems, good ones, among her papers. She even had a flair for catching essentials with spirited, quick pencil sketches, a talent I had not suspected until one day in Alaska after we had been married some twenty years. Something comical in a bear's movements amused her and she recorded the beast's attitude with a few quick strokes. And all these various aptitudes she used merely for her own amusement. It seemed never to occur to her to show them to anyone;

and she was always surprised when I insisted on bringing them out. It was as though they were simply the varied expression of one essential thing within her, so that it did not particularly matter what medium she happened to use. She never took any of them ponderously, nor did she pursue any of them too single-mindedly. But they were part of the "busyness" Of life to which she refers.

And lastly, just for full measure, she did a great deal in social service and charity work—tubercular children, the unemployed before the days of Government relief, and the like.

This for seven or eight months of the year. Summers we cruised, up the Pacific Northwest Coast. As we did our own navigation, and had a vivid side interest in everything from digging clams to chasing after whales, these months also had a considerable "busyness". So when I say that throughout all these twenty years,—from 1919 to 1939,—Betty never failed to find at least one hour every day for this mysterious work to which she was summoned, the strength of its compulsion can be understood.

# 4.

"Remembering the daily anxious messages I had received begging me to go on in the face of discouragement," Betty's own manuscript continues, "I went on with my experiment. There was a lack of my former enthusiasm, however, and this evidently reacted on the communications, which were labored and had not the interest of previous ones. I took up my pencil listlessly, always on guard to repel marauders. In my waning faith I demanded some material proof.

"'Convince me that you are here,' I said. 'Move my arms or legs. Make me feel your presence.' "A sensation ensued of strong currents running through me, but I could not be sure that it was not mental suggestion. Stewart's arms were twisted and jerked around as if he were going through calisthenics and his hands were involuntarily clenched.[6] Immediately I received the following in writing: "'You will not have any success with such manifestations. We do not especially recommend trying them, we are not after that kind of mediumship;

---

[6] Up to this time Betty had, in general, worked alone, with automatic writing. However, I was now "sitting in", as a spectator. The sensation of what she described was similar to the muscle-jerk induced by an electric current.

we want to protect you more or less against just such things and keep our own private wire under proper control and insulation. It may be a comfort and pleasure to feel that way— that we answer and are near— but how can you be sure who it is answering you? It is the cheapest, easiest form of communication. We are building up a different variety for you and your uses. It is a far more delicate mechanism and so more difficult to manipulate. It will, however, be much more reliable.' "We asked the question, 'Who is jerking Stewart's muscles?' "'An experimental pest,' was the answer. Not until sometime later did any involuntary movement of muscles come to me and then it was unsolicited. A rare occurrence.

"Until the beginning of my, second period, nearly a month later, this anaemic uncertain frame of mind possessed me. It may have been due to lack of physical vitality, for I was very tired.

"That I did not abandon the experiment altogether as a dangerous, useless pursuit—as so many do at this period—was partly due to an obstinate disposition and partly to Stewart's interest and encouragement—combined, of course, with that of my spirit family.

Gradually the fog was lifted. By rereading the communications, piecing together bits of advice sent me in regard to control of my own mind and spirit, and by the slow subtle impressions that came to me, I worked out a crude sort of formula for myself. All of a sudden it was successful, and the pall was thrown off me."

# 5.

All I have quoted in the foregoing was written as one piece. Betty's own phrase—"this is written after ten years of constant struggle"— dates it as done in 1929. The internal evidence of the context indicates that she was dealing with only the beginnings, for she had graduated from automatic writing by the first months of 1920. Her training in the technique of receiving and passing on what she was taught and what she experienced, was merely a necessary adjunct to her real job of growth and development. I shall sketch the latter process in due time; but first let us follow out all Betty herself had to say, in her own person.

# CHAPTER 4

# BETTY'S OWN NARRATIVE
# (CONTINUED)

## 1.

In the same file that contained the material embodied in the last chapter I found another manuscript, dealing with the same subject—Betty's beginnings in this job of unfoldment, and how and why she undertook it. The one already quoted was written in 1929. This one must have been done earlier—in 1922. Nevertheless I think they must be read in this reverse order. The emphasis of the 1929 document is on externals, so to speak, while the earlier one deals more with the inner impulses.

## 2.

"For a longtime," this manuscript begins, "there had been an uneasy sense within me of having strayed from the path I desired. I did not try to think it out, I just drifted along.

"During my long wanderings under wide skies, in silent places, the accumulated dust of civilized matter-of-fact life was wiped off. The fresh new surface was more sensitive to reflections from the big simple forces around me, and gradually my old outlook was replaced by a wider vision. It happened quite simply and naturally, without any attitudinizing. I began to grow up.

"Whenever we returned from the isolation of our wilderness travel, I took up worldly affairs with enthusiasm, but each time certain things grew a little less satisfactory and other things vaguely distasteful.

Then came the war to teach us reality.

"After it was over we looked again at our individual lives. I knew the secret of my vague discontent. I had rediscovered the immense possibilities—outside of selfness—in what we vaguely call the spirit. I felt my feet on the road for which I had searched all my life. The vast accumulated experience of the world had, oddly enough, been admitted only to the surface of my mind, and had left little impress on my heart.

Like a child who, with wonder and fascination, discovers that water is wet and that fire will bum, I began my investigations; of the world where lives faith, vitality and the wisdom of the heart—all the big things we live by but cannot analyze in laboratories.

"The first idea that came to me was disconcerting. If I were to die tomorrow, the body I fuss over would leave me, would leave me standing 'as is'? Standing in what? "The awkwardness and unpreparedness of this inevitable situation struck at my imagination. It was too stupid to slouch along in such an improvident unthinking fashion devoid of any purpose, of any inner core which I could retain beyond the moment of this life' "This rather hazy determination to do something about it was strengthened by the stimulation received through automatic writing, which began in the early spring following the armistice. Now for nearly three years I have struggled for comprehension, passing from automatic writing to a curious state of freed or double consciousness in which I absorb experiences directly somehow, and Stewart records them in words spoken through me, or by me as first hand impressions.

"There has been no sudden reformation of my character, accompanied by a firm grip on destiny! During all this time of intensely interesting and puzzling manifestation I had many days of doubt and distraction. I felt like a child walking on stilts—above my usual self, but awkwardly maintaining balance. Only recently has the natural spontaneous happiness of it come to me, and with it a wonderful feeling of firmness inside, somewhere apart from my usual surface consciousness.

"Now let me retrace my steps in this quickening process.

"As I stated, I decided it was high time, and highly desirable and entertaining, to take control of myself. The idea was simple enough, but difficult to carry on. The slothfulness of the human creature is beyond comprehension when we compare it with his latent possibilities. Week after week came the same pleadings in automatic writing before I seriously arranged my busy days to comply.

"'Make up your mind to give up a short time every day to us.' "'Set aside an hour, the same hour, every day.' "'You will need months of practice.' "'It all depends on you and your cooperation.' "'Have you anything more important to do? Ask yourself that question when interruptions threaten and you are tempted to set this hour aside.' "'You will not be able to jump right into success. Do not expect it. It takes much assembling of forces and much elimination by careful experiment.' "'Remember, we can do nothing without your will to reach us.' "'Give us time every day; it is more important than anything else you can do.' "So far nothing startling, but it sounded reasonable; an intelligent beginning. I have found that the only way to learn to shoot a gun, or swim, or acquire any new ability, is by the simple method of shooting or swimming, and *keeping on doing it*. I was interested enough, and curious enough, to try to follow directions, and decided on at least a half hour every single day, without exception.[7]

"Being rather humorously inclined, after making this determination I settled myself and asked politely what I was supposed to do next. My first instructions were in the direction of ordering my mental equipment.

"'Can you manage to be more in the mood and give more time to preparation? It is the only way. You did not have any success before today because your mind was absolutely separated from us by worldly affairs. We are helpless in that case.' "'You must think of us as natural everyday friends who are with you just as others come into your world.' "'Do not strain, nor think of us as supernatural. It is only that your earthly vision is as limited as that of a new-born baby.' "'Be content to let us lead you like a little child, step by step.' "'Drop every worldly, selfish thought. We cannot give you a formula for experiment. It is a case of condition of mind and soul.' "'You must abandon yourself to our method, not confine us to yours. Let it come to you by degrees, naturally, as a plant grows.' "These instructions, and some on relaxing, came sometimes very haltingly, sometimes fluently, as fast as my pencil could travel.

---

[7]   As a matter of fact, the time she thus dedicated averaged much longer.

Always, from the very first, accompanying each instruction, was a sentence or two urging me to do my part.

"It took some time to get into the front of my mind, into my everyday consciousness, just what my part was. It came to me at last as a surprise. It was strengthened will power; though that does not quite express it. Firm substance; resolution, is more nearly it. My part was the holding of myself in control. This was insisted on until I could have no doubt of what was wanted of me.

"I knew how good it felt to have a manageable body.[8] So why stop there? Why not try, as they urged, to get control of the mental and spiritual muscles? Here was training for an exciting new game. I was interested.

There was no use in just sitting and listening. I would do my part, and see what happened next.

"My first effort was disconcerting and slippery, a skiddy performance. What I called my mind refused to stay on the road. Before taking up the pencil I tried, as suggested, to 'prepare my mind.' Every annoyance I had ever experienced, long forgotten, returned to memory to buzz around like diabolical mosquitoes. With persistent effort I banished that annoyance, but its place was taken immediately by an insistent swarm of trivialities of different character. All my pet hobbies and pastimes took possession! It was enough to make one believe in personal devils! "An obstinate Scotch-headedness determined me to do battle for possession of my own mind. Something interesting was being said to me, but my shockingly bad mental manners—squirming, teasing and interrupting—kept me from hearing it. At least I should make myself listen. Then I could calmly decide on the merit of what was being said.

All this traffic of mind must be dodged. The logical course was to make a safety zone in the traffic. I drew an imaginary circle around myself, and stood triumphantly ungettable.

"The pencil began to write fluently: 'When worries and world annoyances come, you can rise strongly and determinedly, spend a few moments in calm, and at once descend, reinforced to the object in hand. Brush away the stinging fly before he sucks your life blood and leaves poison in its place. This alone takes much conscious manipulation to accomplish.

---

[8]  She was a competent sportswoman and no mean acrobat in an amateur way. She could stand on her head, for instance, as easily as a dog sits up. S.E.W.

30

You see I am not giving you noble, difficult tasks to perform. I am only setting a few simple exercises as a point of contact in the beginning. Master these and you will have the vision and strength to see that you are mastering yourself and your destiny.' "'We want to urge you, and keep on urging you, to remember every hour the powers you possess, the forces you have within you to draw upon. Use them in every little thing you do. The degree of success you have depends on the amount of energy put into it.' "It is obvious that each should be big, but of his own volition stays small.' "I shall not quote much further. Day after day I was exhorted to strive for 'habitual consciousness' of unified life. The overwhelming passion of the pleading kindled the commonplace words as I wrote them. Could my own lazy, comfortable subliminal (whatever that may be) stir itself to meet such a frenzy of solicitation for my salvation? As I had lived with it many years and knew only its inertness, the evidence all pointed to an outside force trying to act on my rather reluctant personality.

"The idea of communication was not new to me. In my early childhood I remembered that Grandma Marin and Uncle Calvert had been the butt of the family for professing belief in it. What if all these years they had been trying to reach me and tell me that it is true. This ceased suddenly to be merely an interesting game, and became a matter for serious investigation. I determined to throw more vitality into it; to keep my head steady, but to follow with my heart the possibility that they, my family, were trying to lead me. Whatever it was, I must find out.

"So I continued my daily hour of quiet, with astonishing results. There was never any indication of their taking possession of me in the ordinary sense of overcoming a weak will by a stronger. On the contrary all my experience proves that no spiritual growth is possible without strong control of one's own earth mind; without resolution accompanied by voluntary self-effort and sympathetic enthusiasm. The depth of wisdom and the exceptional technique in developing comprehension of the spiritual life, rather than the evidential material given, forced us to accept the fact that an outside being was directing a systematic course of instruction.

"The old absorption in personal intercourse with friends soon gave way to a bigger scheme. It had to, perforce. As the instruction progressed they[9] developed a lofty disregard of our demands for more entertaining and personal subject matter. It was evidently to be their kind of

---

[9]  The communicators.

thing, or nothing. Our demands for experiments, tests, stunts, manifestations were ignored. This interesting force was not to be bullied. It then occurred to me to assume the part of a rather humble minded eager pupil, and see what such a chastened attitude would accomplish. It accomplished much.

"And so, finally, I bent my energies and interest to trying, from my end, to help the communications as they directed. I experimented with various forms of concentration. I also noted the success or failure of various impulses natural to me. And when these were successful I tried to increase their force, thus evoking my own spiritual vitality. For example: very early I discovered that this vitality was magically successful when reinforced with an outgoing from the heart, as in loving remembrance of a friend.

"This kind of thing, however, I hesitate to emphasize. Formulas are dangerous. Your needs are not my needs. Stability may be the thing I strive for, while flexibility and abandon to spiritual imagination may be the adjustment needed for you. My spiritual strivings may therefore be a misfit for you. You must cultivate your own modeling power to proportion you so that you will attract your own developing currents. These will make you aware of your weak points and aid you in strengthening them through your conscious cooperation until the process becomes spontaneous.

"Above all, get this clear: these notes are intended only to give an example of an individual process, suited to a particular person. Do not let them mummify your own life-giving currents by inducing you to expect anything exactly similar.

"During the years, then, patient experiment has developed in me, together with growing wonderment and faith, a little comprehension of spiritual law. There have been many setbacks, struggles, doubtings. In weak moments I have had an almost cowardly longing for my old comfortably self-absorbed unawareness of life. I emphasize this again because the psychic books I have read describing other people's experiences lay so little stress on the difficulties. Very early I came to look upon these writers as beings of a superior clay, utterly set apart from me. I thought dejectedly how exceptionally unfit I was, with all my failures, my self tortures of doubt, my semi-paralytic state of will. If I did manage to soar serenely, I was sure to flop painfully; and then came the real test of strength in putting myself back. I shall set down the failures and discouragements, even at the risk of clouding the inspiration. We have the records of my shining hours; I shall tell of the slow minutes in between. My own method may be a painfully slow self-evolution, designed for tortoises, and the easy accomplishments of the others are a design reserved for hares, but at least I am determined to arrive some day." (Her intention as to the ultimate use of these notes, I am unable to guess. Whatever it was, she apparently postponed it for the time being.

She adds this:) "The whole subject is much too big for me. What we vaguely, mistily call spiritual, and look at momentarily on Sundays, is as real, natural and joyous as the flesh and blood we accept as a fact of existence. This flesh and blood is the pod for the protection of the ripening spiritual body within us which we inhabit after death. Each of us must *sometime* develop this inner, bigger self. Ours is the choice whether to lie dormant or to start expanding at once from the seed to the plant, and so occupy increasingly more life. It seems to be a case of 'eventually, why not now?' And delay bears compound interest on the amount of effort to be paid out later.

"This concept is as old as the earth itself. We accept it generally as true—but unimportant *at present*; so we are quite content with our half-life. The moment our desire for more life passes from the purely mental into absorption *by our consciousness*, germination begins. If it becomes a fixed habit of mind and *heart*, growth will continue as it was intended to, cooperating with an orderly, useful, practical life.

"We have proved the wisdom and comfort of physical hygiene, why not teach the next generation a little spiritual hygiene? Teach them how to keep their thoughts clean and strongly muscled, to have faith in their healthy impulses, to keep open and expanding hearts. Why not give these their due proportion of acknowledgment and education, along with the development of the brain? Our brains are only the mortal machines we work through, very important as are good, well-oiled typewriters. Why stop education with adaptability to this life? Why not a still higher education? If only for the sake of the full lunged happiness there is in it, teach the next generation youths periodically to lift their eyes from the narrow treads they follow to the wider landscape they may inherit if they will." And she ends on a high note: "The great fact remains," she wrote of herself, "that along with the discouragements has come, in great moments of susceptibility, the setting free within me of a magic genie long bottled up. The expansion of this released, vigorously healthy being has been a happiness beyond anything I imagined possible. The old feeling, too, of being off the road is gone. However it may seem to others, so far as I personally am concerned,

I *know* that I am joyously on my way, just come into my heritage, and longing to share it."

# CHAPTER 5

# BETTY LEARNS TECHNIQUE

Before finally setting out to follow Betty, as well as we can, through the twenty years of her inner expansion, I must describe—very briefly—the mere externals of technique.

The first Ouija board period lasted but a few days. The toy seemed to be used only to attract her attention, and to direct her to a more facile method of communication—automatic writing. Indeed about the only clearly defined "message" it conveyed was the admonition, over and over repeated, "Get a pencil. Get a pencil." I was not present at Betty's first experiments at automatic writing, though of course I saw the results eventually. She described them as slow and fumbling. The first script was ill-formed, without capitals or punctuation or spacing, like one long continuous word. She had to go over it painfully, dividing the words from one another. Sometimes it was necessary to guess at some of them, from the context. But they made such good sense that she brought the scrawls to me. We decided to go on with it.

With practice the writing improved. The words were divided; the letters clearly formed; the sentences capitalized and punctuated. The whole process gained speed and certainty, until it had the facility of one writing a letter about something he really wanted to say. And the content of the instruction thus conveyed was so forward looking and yet so practical, that I settled back in my own mind to much the same anticipation as I would have had in the writing of a book. Here was material; here was the ability to write. What more could one want? And then, after only nine months of it, we were blandly informed that shortly the writing would cease! And it did! We resolved to try a new technique. Betty bandaged her eyes and lay flat. I took her wrist. This was in December 1919.

The experiment was an instant success in that Betty appeared at once to slip easily into a kind of expanded consciousness. Perhaps double consciousness would be better. Her self seemed to be mainly centered in the expansion, but at the same time she retained enough connection with physical existence to talk to me in report of what she saw, heard or did. I think my touch on her wrist was what held this channel open. And I suspect I may, in some mysterious fashion, have contributed to the conditions that enabled her to function in her two aspects at once. At any rate, when she worked alone she brought back nothing for record, though she did report in general even greater personal success. Or perhaps my touch on her wrist was merely her sort of tea leaves or crystal ball—the device that opened the channel. I preferred to think the former. For if my function was only as recorder of what was said, I shall claim a heavenly crown of patience. Even after the technique was established, I was often forced to sit for long intervals, holding Betty's wrist, while she was most happily busy at her own invisible affairs.

But that is a bit ahead of the story. Though from the very first attempt Betty managed this slipping into the double consciousness quite easily, the other aspect—the reporting back—was a different matter. When she tried to tell me about it—whatever it was—her speech was halting, stumbling, fragmentary almost to the point of incoherence. Obscurely, through that incoherence, I thought I caught glimpses of something important. But as compared to our easy, rapid automatic writing this seemed to be a very ramshackle makeshift. Still, I was in it for the duration. Gradually emerged a reasonable explanation. In the automatic writing Betty had been an amanuensis; had merely lent herself as a machine. Now she was to be brought into touch with realities, which she was to absorb and tell about. Also—as herself partaker of this superconsciousness—she would receive direct impressions, would hear words with some "inner ear." While still in the supernormal state, she would bring down these things to that fragment of normal consciousness retained for the purpose, and through it report to me for record.

That was the program, as I understood it, and it seemed both reasonable and interesting. She made quick progress. Soon she was able to tell me matters that made sense in what was gradually revealing itself as an ordered and progressive expansion of herself. And then once more, just as this method in turn began to be really useful, it was interrupted and something new attempted.

We had no warning. On January 28, 1921—almost a year after the first Ouija board trial—Betty withdrew herself into one of her patience—trying private sessions. All I got out of it was a fragment now and then of her side of conversations with her Invisibles—"I'd like to: but can I?" "How silly!" "Where do I find it? Will you show me?"—tantalizing bits.

Finally—after over an hour of this—she turned to me.

"They can't tell me what I'm working toward because they cannot tell yet what I'm capable of developing," said she. "They can't predict: it all depends on me. They want me to do regular laboratory work, but how can I?—How they SHOVE!" she cried. "How they shove me! My, what a force they're putting behind me, pushing me on, on, on!—My other consciousness with you is slipping, slipping—I'm just barely conscious whether I'm talking or not—It's a new phase—I don't want to lose consciousness." She was immobile and silent for thirteen minutes. Then she sighed deeply and slightly moved her feet.

"I can move now. Rouse me. It is all over for tonight. What did they do to me? I was holding intercourse with somebody, but it did not get back to my waking consciousness." I shook her wrist gently, and after a few moments she came back. Whether I liked this or not I did not quite know. But Betty seemed no worse for it. On the contrary, her color was bright, her vitality increased.

The following day's session began again with some private business which wag not confided to me. I gathered that Betty was being persuaded to something. " Oh go ahead; I don't care," she muttered at one time. "I don't know what you're doing," she complained. "Oh, do be definite and don't muddle it!" she cried. "I'm NOT cross! " she disclaimed, "I've got to breathe! " "I don't believe it's going to work anyway," she protested. "—Well, I'll try." Then ten minutes of silence. Suddenly a guttural sound in her throat— GR— , a pause, and the sound was repeated several times, until it extended itself into an almost recognizable word, GRANDMA. After ten seconds, very distinctly and clearly the two words GRANDMA WHITE. But the voice that spoke them was not Betty's! By the same slow and painful process came my love; MANY MORE; the name MARY. And finally the beginning of a sentence, MAKE HER— .

It took just an hour for these few words, with a lot of under—breath rapid comment of protest and apology from Betty. At last she said to me: "Doesn't amount to anything. I wish you'd take me out. I'm tired. It is not coherent, and I cannot help it. They dull me and then do it themselves." After this she continued daily to work—and clearly and valuably—by her old technique of reporting back, from the other consciousness, in her own person, until February 11, when a second attempt was made at what might be called "direct transmission." Here is the entire result of something over an hour.

"Mary—rather hard—realize difficulties—give consideration channel—undeveloped. Progress slow" (came explosively, as one word)"—Sarah—m-mil-militate—aren't you sass" (meant for satisfied, probably) "—don't be so—" Here Betty broke in. "Oh, I'm working so hard! Why do I have to work so hard!" Then, very slowly, with a pause between each word, but clearly: "Method new. No more now. Good night. Wake up!" Nothing happened for five minutes. Then Betty, to Me: "Wake me up. I'm tired—shoving me around that way! I stopped breathing—but I found a new way to breathe. I felt it when it changed. I felt absolutely safe. It isn't uncomfortable unless you stop to think about it. If you don't think about it, you don't have to breathe. Everything swirled and swirled and rocked in a kind of rhythm. I felt myself to be more of a gas substance than flesh and blood. I was; just vaguely conscious of trying to force out something, working very hard." She "awakened" presently, of herself, refreshed, without fatigue.

Nothing further was attempted in the new technique until February 17, though we had the usual sessions in that week. After this manner we continued, using Betty's old technique of reporting back in her own person most of the time, with an occasional laborious period of practice in allowing herself to be used as a mouthpiece. With such practice the difficulty lessened, the facility improved. But nothing important was said that way. Like the first of the automatic writing, the communication was largely personal; a phase almost completely abandoned in the other method.

"We cannot yet—hold it steadily—long enough for subtle explanations—" the Invisible laboriously answered my query as to why this was so. "Your receiving apparatus very primitive—Excuse us!" Not until about the first of May did those in charge consider Betty flexible enough to use for the transmission of anything seriously integral with the main effort. And I should think it fully a year thereafter before the interchange switched back and forth, from Betty in person to Betty as a mere transmitter, freely, without checks and stumbles. Until, in other words, the instrument was perfected.

People have asked me how I knew—outside the context of what was said—when to ascribe to Betty, and when to the Invisibles. Her voice was slightly different in quality and timbre, in the latter case: the phraseology was not of Betty's habit; but the most convincing, and at the same time unprovable, distinction was a decided "feel" of personality. That would, of course, mean nothing to anybody but me; and rarely, when it did not matter one way or the other, I was not myself certain. But ordinarily I was sure.

I have also been asked about physical symptoms, as to Betty's condition while in this state of consciousness.

It was obviously trance, but not complete as in the case of Joan, who actually seems to "go away", leaving her organism to be used. Betty was supposed to work—said the Invisibles—"with intelligent cooperation": I cannot do better than to quote from *The Betty Book* as to this.

"She was to go to them, instead of their coming to her.—And as intelligent cooperation presupposes participation, her consciousness was not taken from her in the customary deep trance. That does not mean that she was conscious as you and I are conscious. She was unaware of her physical surroundings—she went out of her body', as the occultists have it, to some other phase of existence. But in that somewhere else she retained her faculties of thought. She was not put out, drugged. She was transferred—Occasionally, but rarely and only for certain exact accuracies, she goes so 'far away'—as it seems to her—that apparently there remains to her only a shred of (our) consciousness. Bur that shred is always there, and through it the approach to 'intelligent cooperation' is always possible." It took about five minutes for her to become entranced, and about the same time to "come out" after the session was finished. "I'm coming down like a leaf, zig-zag," she once described her return to normal consciousness. I could see no physical change while she was in this state, except that her respiration became almost imperceptible. Nor did she ever suffer any ill after effects, even temporary. None of the nausea, dizziness or the like which some psychics undergo. On the contrary, she always awakened pink-cheeked and refreshed.

Now, having finished the external mechanics of Betty's technical training, we are at last ready to back track, and take up once more her beginnings; but this time from the point of view of the inner consciousness.

# CHAPTER 6

# BETTY TAKES THE ROAD

## 1.

As I look back on these beginnings, I am reminded of the first handling of a skittish colt; and I admire the tact and skill with which the Invisibles did the job. They had, first of all, to get Betty's—and incidentally my—confidence; they must keep our interest; they must persuade her—and me—that the thing was worth doing; and finally must arouse a real desire on her part to go on. In consequence, the early communications were sugar-coated with personal matters; but, with the proportion of the latter gradually lessening, at last the personal was dropped with a finality that resulted in complete anonymity. Only when this was accomplished did they give us a glimpse of their own point of view.

"The content of first messages through new stations,"[10] explained the Invisibles later—six or seven years later; after they had developed Betty as a reliable channel, "is important only as it serves to retain interest and does not discourage by too complete irrelevancy. We are rarely at

---

[10] The Invisibles used the term station—or receiving station—instead of the usual "medium" because, they maintained, the latter has too many connotations.

first attempting to say anything. We are merely trying to get a reaction to stimulus. If this could be fully understood, it would be as effective to convey a single irrelevant word—or indeed mere meaningless sounds. From our point of view the whole importance of a considerably extended period of first work is in the reaction on the part of the station to any impression. Often in a long alleged message a small phrase, a single word, or even a solitary syllable or sound is all that actually emanates from us with definite intent. The rest of the message, so-called, may be a mere going along with what the station himself unconsciously imagines to be the purport." Nevertheless, that bit of genuine response is entirely satisfactory to them, they went on to say, no matter how confused or false or contradictory the whole thing may seem to us. That is because their interest at the moment is in the process, and not in what is said.

However, they admitted, as we at this end know nothing of the process, our interest is naturally in the content, and if that content becomes too nonsensical or unbelievable we are likely to throw the whole thing overboard.

"So," they said, "we give attention to accuracy, or what you call 'evidential,' only when our hand on the pulse of your interest or belief indicates slowing down to a danger point. What we are after is not personal communication, but development of an instrument capable of something more worth while."

## 2.

This was a reasonable and logical explanation of the early puzzlements and bewilderments which Betty touched upon in her own narrative. But it could not be given at the time. She must at first gain her reassurance and encouragement as she could. Her Invisibles were very gentle with her.

"I am a friend," one told her, at the automatic writing stage, "you can trust me. We will uphold and care for you. No harm can possibly come to you. Stewart must not fear for you. We solemnly promise him to guard you. We will make every effort to satisfy him.

"Only hold fast to our love for you and your faith will be justified.

Never mind how discouraging the outlook is, continue to believe us. Do not ask explanations, only believe." And after a particularly confusing series of experiences: "We have not forsaken you, but we are putting you more on your own to work. We do not want to foster dependence on us.

Your unhappiness hinders. Throw it off. You have gone stale from being tired. Rest, and you will regain your outlook. Perhaps we have been too eager and pressed you too hard. Poor little girl, we are sorry for you and would comfort you tonight.—Goodnight, dear. Are you happier now? We are as near you as ever, but we have strained you a little too much. Forgive us." Another time Betty had, evidently, been "getting instruction" beyond her saturation point. She blew up in a burst of laughter.

"So much preaching! " she cried. "I've never been so doggone good in my life! Why, I just ache behind the ears being intelligent! " And then went off in a school-girl giggling fit, renewed every time I tried to ask her anything.

"Now," said the Invisible, when at last she had sobered down, "perhaps you can rid yourself of the very self-conscious attitude we have been trying to point out to you. You were getting to be so busy with your attitude that you could not really listen to us. We are delighted to see you natural again. We do not want any solemn, virtuous-feeling saint in place of a very human little daughter."

# 3.

The too-hard pressure of which they spoke was an unremitting effort to arouse Betty's will to persist. At this time she was far from convinced and was easily discouraged. Ordinarily the stimulus of the Invisibles was gently carried on by appeal to her trust and affection, or to her common sense and self-respect.

"Do you wish to be spiritually illiterate? " they asked her.

Betty did not grasp the connection.

"If we can get it to you, you'll see the point," said they. "When you see a child learning to write, you know how hopeless it looks that it should ever be able to receive inspiration from the printed page. You are in just that stage. But you've got to stick to it. In fact we are going to KEEP you to it. You've got to learn it sometime, just as you had to learn to write. Of course anybody, if he pleases, can remain spiritually illiterate, but then he will have to live a comparatively commonplace existence." I challenged this last. I could not see Betty as commonplace.

"By commonplace we mean keeping your approved boundaries beyond which you make no effort to go. By restricted imagination, by neglect of the unknown—by these you keep yourself commonplace."

"But we have our ordinary daily lives to live," I objected.

"It is not your application to little necessary things we worry about.

It's the UNBROKEN application. That's the thing that makes you commonplace. If you stop work, even drudgery, often enough, and switch your center of consciousness to big spiritual proportions, you can accomplish ordinary life without getting commonplace." This reasonable gentleness, as I say, was the rule. But at times they arose to an almost frantic urgency.

"We lash you to our own frenzy of purpose for your own salvation. Make a vow to us to carry on our work.

We cannot always come with the force of this evening, but we want these words to burn into your soul, to be your obsession, your ruling passion.

Power wanes, and we want to leave you at our highest pitch of urgency, calling to the deeps of you to answer the great duty."

# 4.

Almost from the first hesitantly written words, the Invisibles began to make it clear that they had in mind an important ultimate aim. Betty, it seemed, was to be made an instrument for some purpose not yet defined.

We both possessed a healthy sense of humor, so at first we were inclined to treat such claims with skepticism and some derision. They perilously resembled these super-solemn "especially chosen to bring a Great Message to the World" assurances with which we had become familiar through certain of our acquaintances who had stumbled on "psychics." These experimenters seemed invariably to have been taken in charge by very important people, such as Plato or Aristotle or William James or even Julius Caesar and Nero.

But Betty's Invisibles had proved not to be so high-falutin. They did not pretend to be anybody in particular, and they had not as yet offered any Message. It was merely that they had a purpose in training her, which was not so unreasonable when we stopped to think of it.

"It's only," said they "that we're giving you a little encouragement that you are more than a mere bystander taking notes. It's not a futile task. Once the inter-relation of all created things is even dimly sensed, one cannot again be small. The mantle of magnitude is over the most humble part of the whole." What they wanted, they kept on repeating, was to teach Betty how to expand her consciousness. As a result, said they, she would become permeable to the invisible spiritual forces from which ordinary life insulates us more or less. This, for lack of a better term, they called Contact with the Source. Incidental to it would come an improved type of this thing they were now doing so imperfectly—communication from their world to ours.

"We have been a long time planning this," said they, "so do not fail us.

This is a great experiment for us. Much depends on you. It is the usual thing to have a person surrender all initiative as soon as we establish communication. We want you to gain strength from us, not lose it and become dependent. Involuntary mediums are good only as long as the conditions suit them—a voluntary medium in full control would be invaluable. We do not want to be too strong on this side because it is part of our scheme to have you do your share. We can write pages very fluently and easily when we wish, but it is safer to make you an active agent instead of a passive one." It was about this time, I believe, that they dropped the word MEDIUM as too full of connotation, and adopted the word station instead. About this time, also, Betty resolved to give these supposed Invisibles a "sporting chance."

# 5.

The expansion of consciousness desired by the Invisibles turned out to be no simple task. Betty devoted an hour or so each day to following directions as best she could. But this, she herself confessed, was not very successful, for she could not make out just what was wanted of her.

At first she struggled for a complete, clear-cut intellectual picture—largely, I think, so she could satisfy me. But the Invisibles rejected the mental approach.

"How can we bring to you strongly enough," said they, "the first principle of what we want you to do? It is to expand IN SPIRIT, not intellectually. The spirit is usually like a desiccated fruit inside the brain. We fear to give you too much for that reason. You are too much in your brain. Let your spirit soak up in a simple and pleasant fashion until it is a fitting mate for your brain." Such expansion, they asserted, would in due time result in the development of an entirely new faculty.

"It is like learning another language," said they, "so you can listen to us with understanding. Each time you desire to travel beyond your present country you must say to yourself: am I thinking and listening in the right language? Otherwise communication is hopeless." There was a pause; then Betty said faintly, "I'm going away off now." "This faculty," resumed the Invisibles presently "which we awkwardly call listening, thinking in another language, is an expansion of the progressive reality within you. You must strive for possession—as a subconscious fixture—of a faculty not sufficiently developed in you yet.

Until you can absorb knowledge directly with this faculty, you will always be subject to dilutions, contaminations, dispersions.

"This absorption of comprehension, only partial of course, carried through the present channels of contact, arrives transmuted from the reality of the source into the symbols of the brain. It is almost useless to attempt much further extension of vision until you work out this faculty for receiving direct comprehension. The brain is a physical apparatus. It will always automatically take what it is able to absorb.

But the inner expansive faculty, vigorously developed, can outrun the physical apparatus indefinitely." There was a short pause.

"It is so discouraging," ended Betty, "now I see that double image at the water's edge—reality and reflection. They look just alike, but they are so different! I get the reality and take hold of it; but I only give you the reflection."

# 6.

Betty was really working very hard to do her share well and conscientiously. In fact, as it turned out, she tried too hard.

"Don't strain in these efforts," warned the Invisibles. "Keep the body relaxed, but free and stimulate the spirit to respond with a great and rising wonder, similar to that inspired by the overwhelming beauties of nature. Unstopped your imprisoned spirit; let it rise blithely and naturally. Enjoy yourself. Don't strain. Let your heart dominate, and abandon yourself to its impulses. You will release yourself from terrible intellectual bonds: terrible, however, only when unbalanced." "We want none of the usual abandoning yourself to outside influences," said they at another time. "It is all a matter of holding yourself together around a good firm core of aspiration and interest and aim as to where you are headed.

"And one more tip we want to give you," they added. "Run hard from the curiosity seekers who will try to make a gymkhana out of you. Don't let them even have a look in. Tell 'em anything you like, but head 'em off, for they will queer the whole thing in your mind if you will let them.

In time you will have many clamoring after your help, but you must make them seek for themselves, not attach themselves to you like leeches." These and similar warnings were repeated again and again. They insisted that the usual morbid curiosity in "psychics" led to a by-road, or blind alley, from which Betty must be blocked.

And another tendency of which she must be cured was over-eagerness. That was a natural mistake—once her enthusiasm was aroused for this fascinating exploration. The Invisibles gave her some kind of a jarring, I don't know what it was. I knew there had been something startling going on. I asked Betty.

"You see," she told me, "I was just slipping over when something happened, just at the wrong moment, and checked me back too suddenly.

And I was so disappointed, so eager to go on, that I flung myself back absolutely wide open, tried to get myself back by an enthusiastic abandon, and that stopped the performance. That's what brought down on my head this warning stuff. No more going ahead under these false and dangerous conditions."

# 6.

"False and dangerous conditions—"—we had thought only vaguely of that aspect. And we had taken it for granted that we were going ahead, that we were on our way. Hadn't we agreed "to give them a sporting chance"? But to our surprise—to mine at least—it seemed that was not enough. We must actually enlist; and of our own free will; and with a plain statement of decision. Apparently we had not been called upon for it until sufficient demonstrations had provided materials for intelligent choice. Well, now we had them. And the Invisibles squarely called a halt.

"Escape," they pointed out, "is not merely getting free. It is taking up responsibilities." "Before going on with us," they continued, "certain facts must be faced.

You must pay a price to serve our cause. If you are to succeed, you must go into training. Are you willing to do it? We do not intend to interfere with normal life, but you must consecrate your spiritual life to us, and conserve its vitality and composure.

"Perhaps this work, if undertaken, will lead you into paths you do not wish to tread, but once started you cannot choose. You must take all or nothing, so do not draw back if we lead you to the edge and tell you to look. You will be tried in the fires of experience to see if you are fit to endure." This, I myself considered, must be Betty's decision, not mine. I felt that the expansion she had already gained must have sharpened her intuition to a sufficient wisdom. But secretly I reserved the right of veto should this mysterious warning uncover in her mind the slightest alarm or hesitation. She considered it carefully. "I can stop where I am," mused Betty, "where nearly everybody stops—with the comfortable crowd. But the compliment has been paid me of an opportunity to surmount normal boundaries, to accept the unillumined path of apprenticeship, wrenching myself free... Oh, the cost of the wrench!" What the "cost of the wrench" would be she did not disclose, nor did I confuse the issue by inquiry. Questions sometimes make cross currents.

"It is life," she reflected. "And I want to get nearer, nearer to the source of all striving life. I want to smell the wet earth and feel the cool drip of rocks. I want to sway with the presence of the wind. That is all life, life...

"I want to keep close, close as I can get, to that. I want to sniff it, taste it, drink it, bathe in it. That's where I want to be. I don't like the dead things. Some people like intellectual conquest, mechanical things, making automatons; but I don't like that, I crave the live things; things endowed with self-structure.

"I want to get near enough so I can partake of the same great vitality. Throw open all hatches. I want to go out in the wind and the light and the air. I don't know what you call that current of vitality...

Never mind its name; I'm going to get close to it!" She fell into a long period of deep reflection. Suddenly she decided.

"Give me all of life before I leave!" she cried passionately. "All! All! I don't want a niche. Aren't there plenty of people to fill niches? Of course, they are happier in the peace of limited struggle. But I want most tremendously and vehemently the highest possible comprehension! I want to take the suffering and all! I don't care if it tears me to bits; I want it! I've made my choice. I don't care if it is hard. It isn't all suffering. The intensification of living is worth it." She had set foot on *The Road I Know.*

# CHAPTER 7

# "SEEK AND YOU SHALL FIND"

## 1.

From this high peak of exalted dedication the Invisibles yanked Betty down to consideration of the practical—rather humorously, I thought. All very well splendidly to defy unknown dangers. Any hero can do that! But how about the minor everyday penalties? "They're afraid I minimize the price," Betty told me.

"The price?" I queried.

"Solitude of association," said she, "—but I'm willing to pay it." I was still dumb, so they diagrammed it like this: Nobody enjoys being considered "queer," I was told; and what was going to be the use of all Betty's great effort unless she came into the open eventually, and applied it in the world of daily living? The prospect did not dismay her, though it made her a little sad.

"What a pity if my friends misjudge me," she regretted. "They could withdraw so much of the nice, warm human interchange. I know there will be an assault of misunderstanding. They'll all be critical, I'm afraid; watching me in a suspicious way. It will be hard for me to rise above their attitude and work unaffected by it. Well, I know there's a price.

There is so much disapprobation of boundary-breakers." She considered the situation.

"Well, now we've settled that," she went on, after a while. "I'll think over how to repel impertinence with some dignity and conviction of superiority, and not merely withdraw, or combat in lower terms and with lower weapons...

"I know what I'll do—I've a right to my own life. I won't get combative or superior or scornful; I'll get CONFIDENTIAL. I'll say: "'Well, I'll tell you. A few times in my life I've seen treasure trove, something that had nothing to do with money, or position, or fame, or anything else I can name, but just a deep, powerful sort of happiness, and possible to obtain too; and I'm going to get it if I search through every law, sacred and profane, until I find it. Wouldn't you like to have it? Wouldn't it be worth living if you got track of it, even if you did make mistakes? "'Well then, leave me be: I'm exploring. If I find it, i'll let you know.

In the meantime I am discovering many by-products well worth the having, well worth the effort of discovery. We all want happiness; but I don't want the passive kind. I want big, powerful, creative happiness, and I want it all packed up and ready to take with me when I die" "That's the way I'll talk to them. I'll just take them into my confidence as to what I am after. And it's the truth, and that's all there is to it." An excellent attitude of mind, but the Invisibles seemed not certain that she even yet understood what she might be up against.

"You see," they said, "everything one does for self-development—awareness, expansion, contact and all the rest—has a certain acceptability to the ego concerned, and nobody objects. But when you reverse that, and begin to insist on outgo, offering something of your own attainment, testing it against the world's resistance and misunderstanding, then you must expect a harder time. It is one thing to have a neat chapel to visit occasionally, and quite another to carry its influence into 'practical' life." And, said I, while an attitude of mind helps fortitude, it does not protect from suffering.

"Sensitiveness capable of absorbing wisdom through direct impression suffers enormously from the world of combat," the Invisibles agreed.

"For as awareness increases, so does suffering. Because of this, unfortunately, the spiritual aspirant often prefers to seek a sheltered life and become a bystander. Such a person may have an exquisitely sensitized vision, but he is absolutely sterile because of lack of human contact. The bystander probably regards his reaction as one of fastidiousness, but it is really inertia, atrophied force, over-cultivation, loss of productiveness." Betty recurred to a picture they had seemed to be showing her.

"I want to look at that chap again," she begged. "He's quite fascinating, quite exquisite but useless. If he were set in action, so much of him would break or crumble or change. What a pity he couldn't be used! He's such a highly developed specimen." "The whole point is," insisted the Invisibles, "any sensitive person is useless in employing the force of the higher consciousness if he is always vulnerable to the return blows of the world. Suppose he is trying to accomplish something, and everybody begins irrelevant personal attacks, obstructions of all kinds. The minute he becomes susceptible to all that he is automatically shut off from the power-current which was going to HELP him accomplish.

"You yourself must look out for this. You have gained access to a shining substance. Now you must learn to use it against a lower element superior in quantity. The toughening process which will make your bit of strength available must rest with you. Little by little, in small matters at first, you must learn to protect your mind against the darts and arrows which poison resolution." "Hardihood," commented Betty. "That is a nice word. It just happened to come around." "No suggestions are offered today," concluded the Invisibles. "The problem is merely stated for your solution. You stand at the crossroads.

Either you proceed faintly shadowed by a strange experience, or you strive onward toward a hold on the vitality of spiritual life which will remain unbroken even in your darkest hours.

"Better think it over," they warned.

As I look back I doubt if the Invisibles anticipated that Betty would encounter any considerable degree of criticism among, friends and acquaintances because of her interest in psychic development. As a matter of fact she met almost none. They were testing her only, am sure.

# 2.

Very well, the Invisibles told Betty, in effect, when she failed to be impressed by their warnings, if you are really going on with this thing, you must first of all realize that mere assent is not enough. "There is," said they, "no suction quality to passive willingness. We cannot start things, that part of it is your job; we can merely complement your own effort." And—they added this impressively for Betty's own instruction—it must be done by your own "heart-desire and not mind-desire." They made much of this point: it was all-important.

"It is useless just to sit with mental preparation," said the Invisibles. "You must have the soul preparation, too—the spirit, not the letter of the law. As soon as you have yourself established the right condition, we can come. That is why we are trying to go only as fast as you can assure your own grasp and accomplishment. Otherwise we would be taking you from useful things of the world into a no-man's land of idle speculative dreaming. This is far from our purpose. When you do not succeed, seek the reason in yourself. Your surface mind may be going through certain evolutions which have no growth or corresponding demand from within. In that case you are not truly seeking; you are apathetically making an appeal which has no power behind it to accomplish." They continued, over many sessions, to return to this concept, and ever the more strongly.

"Only steadfast determination and striving will bring you the step further you must go. It is all in your hands now. We can do little more than watch you gain this necessary strength before we can help further.

That is the law. We may advise and influence, but you must make selection and experiment.

"ALWAYS HOLD IN MIND HOW MUCH DEPENDS ON AROUSING YOURSELF. The energy with which you demand of us will measure what you get. It is not the energy of commanding, but of showing the force which begets its complement. It is the energy of measure for measure, given and received.

This is all very indefinite to you now, but remember you are experimenting with forces not recognized in your world of sense." "What do you mean by unrecognized forces?" I demanded. It seemed to me highly desirable to know with what we were supposed to deal, for I was still in somewhat of a doubtful frame of mind. My query caused some hesitation.

"Let us call the whole a matter of inspirational force, for the sake of giving it a name," was the reply. "It comes from a combination of conditions created by the person himself. We only take advantage of this combination. Once a person of his own choice established it, we can act on it. The initial step is your work. We hesitate to use words like soul-yearnings, for instance, because in your mind they have a set significance. But the idea is that we cannot work on an unreceptive person in any satisfactory degree. Roughly speaking, the forces we use are emanations from you. They meet complementary forces not your own that unite with them and so open up a further process of creative selection."[11] A little later they summed up very neatly this necessity for more than acquiescence.

"It is just by determination and faith," said they, "that you accomplish the first dead lift. That manifestation with yourself and by yourself, you must get before you gain any response. This is what people do not realize. They don't put any strength into it, and when it will not work at once, they go the other way. You must get that strength for yourself." Another point on which the Invisibles insisted was that Betty must make haste slowly.

"Do not look on this thing that we want you to do," said they, "as something that can be accomplished in a year or two. Think of it as for eternity. You are stronger than we hoped, and we can go faster than we expected, but we dare not strain you too far. A few simple tasks at a time are all we ask. You will soon see the plan and be impatient to go faster, but you must not try to fly until you are sure of your wings. We prefer to keep you a little clipped until we are surer of your endurance. Some day we will take the air together and all your work will be rewarded. Meanwhile break down your barriers; let in the flood of spirit we are sending to you. Welcome it and feed upon it greedily.

Remember every waking moment to be really trying to live according to the few rules we have given. You will understand better as you go along.

"Above all," they cautioned, "do not strain for psychic power, dividing and disintegrating your force. Rather weld together. Hold yourself a responsible being, capable of limitless possibilities, and so lift up your spirit healthy and whole, asking to be stimulated to greater effort.

"Don't you see, the instant you try to create, to pump up, to reach for definite things, you are in grave danger. You will never get anywhere if you are thinking of what you are going to get. In that case you would be just a curiosity seeker along with so many other people! "Belief in the attainability of higher powers is a legitimate ambition, but such powers must be grown into faithfully. Meanwhile simply lay bare your problems to the influence of the great expansion, which will bring your solution. This is the only real channel which will bring permanent wholesome psychic influence. It is the safe and open highroad. There are other ways, of course, but they are exploration."

---

[11] Those who have read *The Unobstructed Universe* may find in this last a foreshadowing of the truly great theory of creative selection there set forth.

# CHAPTER 8

# THE INNER CITADEL

Shrinking from being misunderstood may be only one way of thinking too much of one's self.

"The first line of attack here," said the Invisibles when in due course they did get around to suggestions, "has to be in the direction of elimination. And that implies a deliberate inspection of egoism and coming to terms with it. Always you are dealing with the ego. You desire generous and spontaneous blending with other lives, but there is a toughened membrane—call it the ego—which obstructs that blending.

"Now in place of this toughened membrane of an ego—which can be wounded, and is sadly scarred by contacts with life—we substitute an indestructible self, a self held together by intention, and by cooperation with universal force; a self vastly more flexible, permeable and self-controlled." This substitution of a non-ego self proved to be no mere figure of speech.

At the next session the Invisibles resumed the discussion. It was in process very simple, they protested. You do withdraw yourself, in a sense. There is in every individual, they told Betty, an inner citadel, a "Psychic core." "It is his enduring center, his seed that will endure." Search yourself, they urged her, for this constant within. And then consciously establish it.

"You will not find it in your brain," they said. "Look for it rather in the region of the heart; or more accurately the intangible sensations that have no organic position. This is the great security, the foundation for any superstructure of effort you may want to build.

"The first step in control is the recognition of such an inner fortress for protection and refreshment. There is nothing more important than creating this abode of emotional security, spiritual order and demonstrable strength.

"You see, the great question is: how are you going to stabilize yourself among all the shifting pursuits of the world, the varied points of view, the conflicts and uncertainties? How are you going to reach reality in the midst of them? And the only answer is, first to make within yourself an individual bit of reality over which you have complete jurisdiction. That is your one method of approach to the ultimate attainment of complete reality." A fine blueprint but a large order, thought I. Very simple. For Betty! First you establish the inner citadel, and then establish yourself in it. Then from it, as headquarters, you act.

"The top layer is much the nicest place to establish yourself," Betty volunteered. "You can look at all your troubles, humorously and in proportion, as most objectionable mosquitoes, but still as only mosquitoes, and yourself as outlasting them. That's the way to live." "Things surge beneath, picking and battering and fuming, but cannot destroy you," the Invisibles took it up. "As long as you have this inner power you needn't mind what is battering against you, nor what tools or dynamite are used. Such can be only a surface nuisance. The shell may be scarred, but you have withdrawn the part of you that can be hurt.

"Take your moments of discord and entanglement," they challenged. "How are you going to possess yourself? "There is only one way, but you must have prepared it beforehand and practiced it: let go your hold of everything and withdraw into the magic-working center of life within yourself. It is always possible to check your nervous reactions momentarily by suddenly commanding a relaxation, like making yourself stop shivering. Then quickly combine this momentary release with a swift retreat to your inner citadel. Go apart in it and rest the tensions. Stay in peace and quiet of volition, acquiescing in your whole being to the reharmonizing power of your higher consciousness. It is to your ordinary faculties as is an adult sympathetic mind to a child's troubles. It helps you clarify your vision and gather strength to make your decisions and plan your actions." And, they added, it is a sure refuge when outside pressure threatens really to overwhelm. Then is justified the complete withdrawal for recuperation. Betty caught at this aspect, considering it for some time before reporting it to me.

"When too weak for aspiration, too sick for effort," she said at last, "what would I do to get buoyant again? Huddled down, hating my own darkness; the divine spark imprisoned, held captive; the physical shackled—I don't like it, but what to do? "I'll burrow down still further inside myself. I'll lie in close to the divine spark imprisoned there. Weary-hearted, I'll acknowledge my plight. Achingly I'll unite with the light that I know is there. Nothing else. No expectancy; no hurry. To my quiet relief, even amid aching inharmony, harmony must rush to succor.

"That sounds pretty abstract, I know, but it really is the process in zero conditions." "But," Warned the Invisibles, "do not forget that if you would progress, you must inevitably go forth again to take your full share of the buffeting of the elements. This, however, does not mean that you are called upon to plunge heedlessly into the muck and mire. Do what comes, bear what comes in natural course, but do not overweight beyond what your serenity is capable of floating. Distinguish between withdrawal and hearty but undamaged living." The session was about over, so Betty did not pursue the subject then; but she caught the point. "I am coming out now," said she, "and the reality is getting thinner and paler. As I drift away from it, all I can be sure of is that it is not enough to say with great dignity: I withdraw my consciousness. That is no good. A dignified withdrawal from earth frets looks rather silly!"

# CHAPTER 9

# IN-FLOODING STRENGTH

## 1.

I must confess that the early period of Betty's instruction was a tough one for me. I see now that she was being given the basic foundations, and that some of them—like the "Inner citadel," for example—had to be given content before they could become practical. But at the time the teaching was—to me—merely a point of view. It was fragmentary; it was vague; it came slowly. For her part Betty was enthusiastic. But she was having the experiences; I wasn't. All I did was to sit there for an hour or so, with pencil and paper, taking down what little there was to take down. A great deal of the time nothing was said by anybody. I patted myself on the back for being so long suffering. Now I see I might have made a positive contribution through some kind of enthusiasm of my own; but the Invisibles themselves realized that this was a good deal to ask on the basis of what was offered me.

"You are very patient," they told me appreciatively one day, "— and that is all," they added dryly.

My job was distinctly sideline sitter; and recorder; of course. I listened to directions given Betty as to processes unseen by me— "Too expectant— not enough relaxed." "You are striving so much to make your mind receptive that you defeat our purpose and open your mind to other sources." "We have decided on a slight change of plan for you. We are going to make you put in practice as nearly as possible each phase as you acquire it. Roughly the plan is this: we will lead you into our world for your lessons, but in order to obtain any further instruction you must do your practicing at home. We are not trying to lead you away from world experience, only to strengthen and enlighten you about it." "Open up more naturally, and do not keep such a stern hand on yourself and your emotions. It won't harm you if you go to the opposite extreme for a while until balance is gained." "Now try to regulate your breathing: several short quick breaths and a long one, and then let go. One after the other. When you breathe do not strain for anything. Try to forget that part. Just go in and out with the tide." "We are putting you through a time of slow preparation, and you are not standing still, as you think... At present you are necessarily muscle-bound in your mind with too much effort." "Push. Push through as you would in walking against a strong wind." That sort of thing. Stage directions. Of a drama that I, in the wings, could not see. Once in a long while the Invisibles tossed me something personal, a bit of "evidential," a brief explanation. As a fish is tossed to a trained seal.

Betty herself realized that her reports back were incomplete.

"Are these words right?" she asked me, rather anxiously. "They did not get laid just right... Words! Words! Words! " She cried, exasperated. "We have to string boundaries of them around even the dimmest comprehension. And more is there than can ever be contained!" But right then the Invisibles apparently did not care whether or not there was any mental comprehension—in either of us. They weren't interested in our minds. Minds came in later, they assured us.

"It is the amateur method to seek growth or spiritual freedom," said they, "by an intense concentration of mind; but this must be replaced by expansion of the heart. That reestablishes the proportion of spirit over the material, and welds the being into a new functioning body capable of volition. There is a great difference between the terrible diffusions of seeking occult power and the expansion of the heart which arranges your proportions and makes you a workable reality. You are past the first danger posts. Do not wonder at silences on our part. Daily strengthening of purpose by silent contemplation of your intention, that is what we have been trying to lead you to, not to daily seeking for adventure."

# 2.

Nevertheless even I could perceive certain definite steps of instruction.

The first thing Betty was to accomplish was permeability to the invisible spiritual forces, or Contact with the Source. The result of this was to be spiritual consciousness. At first she gained it only in touches, flashes.

Next she must extend the duration of spiritual consciousness until it became habitual. Once she was able to transfer her headquarters for living from her old limited, earth consciousness to this expanded consciousness, she must learn how to utilize her new vantage point, and her new powers and insight, in her ordinary conduct of life and her relations to the people about her.

That, stripped of all technique, was the program. And its emphasis on mundane utilization; the immediate application to life, not to some impractical mysticism, gave it common sense to me. The ultimate aim, the fashioning of Betty as an instrument for work after she had left earth life, was not then apparent to us.

None of this burst upon Betty all at once, as an "illumination." The idea and the practice of Contact was introduced to her gradually, as one might teach a beginner to swim. One day she had been quiet for much longer than usual. I began to get restless.

"What are you up to?" I demanded at last.

"Getting porous," Betty replied. "Porosity..." She paused to savour this, then chuckled. "That's a nice fat juicy word! It sucks in and out.

"When you are cold and enter a room, a warm room, you say to yourself that you are in a different atmosphere, and instantly expand to it. That is the difference between ordinary life and the element I'm in." "What element? " I tried for even a glimpse of understanding.

"It's a new medium of sensation," she explained, "the most relaxing and yet vigorous state you can imagine—so abounding in beauty and vitality.

It's too wonderful for me to grasp just yet." "Can't you tell me more of this new medium?" "Could you imagine a substance made out of spring? " she replied. "Not of individual fresh willows and buds and blossoms and tender greens and bursting colors—not those details, but the very sweep of an entire world decked out; the SUBSTANCE of Spring. Don't you see how fresh, delicious, exciting, exalting it would be compared to ordinary things? I am in this superlative beauty and freshness and exquisite delicacy. It is hard to describe in clumsy terms, or name anything but just the 'substance of spring.'" Which sounded pleasant and poetic, but those were the days when I was pragmatic and still somewhat skeptical. For satisfaction I wanted both reasons and results. Nevertheless I held my fire and awaited developments. Much instruction followed, whose purpose I fathomed not at all. For example: "We would like you," the Invisibles speaking through Betty told her, "to cultivate to the utmost your instinct for beauty: form, poems—anything that has been achieved by man in his brief moments of triumph and contact with the over-soul. It is the biggest uplifting material thing you can possess... Do not be afraid to drink deep of beauty. It is an open door through which you can glimpse what is to come: beauty, all that is harmony and in opposition to discord. Beauty is a great and quiet teacher. Detailed education is very important, but it is beset with many restrictions and pitfalls. It is a wise teacher who keeps his pupils looking at the end of the vista instead of watching their feet on the narrow path they walk." To me, sitting on the sidelines, that sounded a good deal like urging Betty to be Betty! But day after day they kept her at whatever lay behind their words.

"Beauty and love," they insisted. "You hear us say love so often that the word ceases to convey any idea to you; but it is the all-containing, permeating essence which will unite your world to ours. We wish we had another word for it. But we see it as the first principle of growth.

Open the flood gates, let the great current of the universe pour through you to others, if you would live."

# 3.

Much of Betty's instruction was given in this mood of poetic imagery.

Again the Invisibles would express themselves in what seemed to me more practical terms.

"Don't try for anything," said they on one occasion, "but just the feeling of a substance as physically permeating as ether or gas or something like that. Try simply, in relaxing, to feel that this substance permeates every inch of your body. Accustom yourself to the feel of it. You will find it will rest you and bring happiness even in the very beginning. You have tried it before; but this will visualize it. Do it at any time; momentarily. It's an actual fact, this inlet of strength." There was a pause, evidently for experiment.

"Anybody could do it," said Betty presently. "It is a matter-of-fact law. I don't see anything 'psychic' about it. I am just studying the law;

and little by little I am demonstrating it. The biggest thing you can study is this permeating strength, and how much of it you can take.

I lie here and strive according to the poor little rules I have discovered already, and something like a slight chemical change takes place that makes me aware of my own possibility. I am just a poor feeble beginner, but I can see so much ahead." "Here are the only tasks we give you now," concluded the Invisibles, "first, love-attract unselfishly; second, as we told you before, walk through your days as a creature with folded wings, conscious of the possession of another element and of your ability to enter it; third, live enough in spirit to invite inspiration, and act promptly without questioning on what comes to you.

For a while Betty seemed to be considering this. Then she said: "I feel like Columbus after weeks and weeks of travel, holding fast to the faith that it's there on the other side. I mustn't relax that faith."

# 4.

Betty's faith was not ill-founded, but also its fulfillment was not immediate. Other things in her makeup delayed matters for a time.

Notably caution. Betty was far from being credulous or an easy mark. Her long line of Scotch ancestors had given her a certain hard-headed skepticism. At the time it seemed to me a mighty useful trait in this kind of a job. It still does. But also its use could be overdone. The Invisibles pointed this out.

"Don't be afraid to accept your dreamland," they advised her. "You have enough ingrained practical, habits to bring you back to balance whenever necessary, but unless you let go your present control you will never be able to do our work. The fact that you have that control is your greatest asset if you can turn it off at will and control it. Do you see what we are doing? Step by step we are trying to break the bonds which tic you down to your earthly village and help you to enter the wider world we live in. Yes, it is like getting you off sticky flypaper. You want to do it, but you must conquer your bodily instincts and habits first. You have the imagination and control but the abandon must be acquired." Betty must have been able to obey orders, for shortly she reported: "I am being taken along with some Strong Ones. Their association invigorates me so. I am going through some kind of an experience on a higher level. Before, I was like a little skinny chickabiddy thing that refused to come out of its shell-crouched in its little shell because that was all it knew that was comfortable. Now someone is helping me to step bravely out and I am feeling strong and sure, and not regretting the sacrifice of my shell." "You can have little conception now of the intense happiness toward which you are progressing," the Invisibles encouraged her. "We don't want to ENTICE you with statements that—misconceived—would endanger a simple approach to the reality. But no inner vision must ever have a wall instead of a horizon." For some little time Betty was silent. Then she announced: "I've always before stuck my head up through a hatchway and tried to look around; but now I've climbed up. I'm all here but I don't know what to do." She chuckled.

"This is a great game—a great game, I tell you what! Like a fairy story. . . . My, but this is the life! Again she was silent.

"Well, I've got to do something about it now. I can't just stand and say how nice it is. All the old ideas and sensations are under-foot, as though I had taken off my clothes and were standing on them ready to swim... But what'll I do?" "Never mind," said the Invisibles, "just go on." "You must have brought me here for some reason," Betty insisted. "What is it? I'm listening." Once more the interval of silence. Then she laughed.

"Supposing," she began, "just supposing you suddenly found yourself free as air, released into the bigness of the solar system as compared with the earth. Supposing you were just jumping with energy and eagerness and enthusiasm, and the only danger seemed to be spreading out too wide and maybe dissolving yourself. And if you had no plan about what you'd accomplish with all that bursting energy—That's just my trouble now.

Generally people make plans first.

Then, when the plan is big enough, energy is meted out. But here I am, all dressed up in energy, and no place to go! I don't know what to do first. It's too big. . My inwardness isn't big enough for it. I want to give it to you—lots of it. Maybe that's the reason it is given to me." She contemplated this for a moment.

"If I could only thicken it up a little," she mused, "so you could use it." There was a short pause. Then, sadly: "I can't thicken it up enough!" "The general trend is toward a more spiritual life," hinted the Invisibles.

"All right," I put in my oar, "what is 'spiritual'?" "It is just daily life carried on by a self with higher associations," was the answer. "That daily life can either go on growing, or be dwarfed and stand still. When it is dwarfed, you are not conscious of it, just as you are not conscious of an atrophied organ. When it begins to grow it takes possession of you and pushes other things aside.

"You'll see the point, in time," said the Invisibles, addressing Betty.

"All you can do at present is to embody, in your daily life, your aspiration and kinship with the stars. Above all be patient. Go about your affairs and do not expect us unless we manifest. We are lifting you. Play and laugh and love and work to rise. Cannot you feel even now that you have set a little harder task for yourself and that you can see a little farther?" In other words, she must first absorb the concept—whatever it was—and then understand it. But understanding, in the Invisibles' definition, seemed to be something more than mere mental appraisal and judgment. It was a kind of incorporation into the substance of one's self. The Invisibles called this "MAKE-IT-SO," borrowing the phrase by which a navy officer makes official a happening aboard ship. "You must not only understand it, but you must make-it-so before it is your possession," the Invisibles summed it up.

# CHAPTER 10

# INHERITING THE LAW

## 1.

**M**any different primary phases were mixed in with the first development of the idea of Contact. In addition to the inner citadel, there were, for example, such things as insulation, elimination of undesirables, and a half dozen other technicalities fully treated in *The Betty Book*, but out of place here. That is what I meant when I said that to me at this time the instruction seemed fragmentary. As far as I was concerned the lack of sequence was maddening. The Invisibles would bring up a brand-new topic of instruction or discussion; would get my interest just nicely started on it; and then drop it in favor of something entirely different. They gave things in dabs. Sometimes they had four or five subjects going at once. Talk about keeping track of a three ringed circus! I have—or had then—a tidy mind.

"Why don't you finish a thing once you've begun it? " I complained, "instead of romping around like the giddy goat!" I got no exact answer at the time; but I had ceased expecting exact answers to that type of question. To answer would have been, I suppose, to defeat the very purpose of the indirection. In other words, arousing too directly the interest of Betty's subconscious mind would have resulted in what we called "coloring"; which means that the said subconscious would take over, more or less, and inject its own ideas. In the early stages of Betty's training this had to be carefully guarded against. After about five years, however, such precaution was no longer necessary. Betty herself had command; and the "sub" had not a look-in.

Then, to my satisfaction, the little-dab method was abandoned. That was one answer to my question. There was another, but the Invisibles gave it only after Betty had gone beyond the need for that technique.

"For purposes of study there is over-magnification of a part," they now told me. "To avoid misstatement there must be occasional pauses to contemplate this magnified part in relation to the whole. That is, the part must be shoved back and diminished to its proper relationship. The constant changing of subject to which you have always objected is the only method we could devise of accomplishing this purpose. It allowed the picture to retire to its proper proportions."

That satisfied my mind. An unusual concession on the part of the Invisibles. For a long time they *seemed* to have almost a contempt for intellect. That proved not to be really so. Merely, for the moment, the intellect was not the appropriate tool; and moreover as a usual thing, in our ordinary processes, we use the intellect almost exclusively, forgetting the non-intellectual—shall I say intuitional—equipment which now the Invisibles wished to bring up to correct balance. But, as usual, they did not explain this until the fact was accomplished; and that one thing came nearer throwing me off the whole business than anything else.

My life had been one that required a very active use of the intellect.

And if my, mind could not endorse a thing, then it was out, as far as I was concerned. Now, apparently, I was being asked to accept things without that endorsement! I say apparently, for later I found out this was not at all what they were asking. I understood, finally, that I was not to set aside intellectual judgments: but merely to postpone them until the accomplished fact. Then I could use my mind as critically as I pleased. Indeed, the Invisibles wanted me to do so! The whole thing boiled down to one simple statement: the brain is the executive, not the originating, branch of our personal government.

Why did they not tell me this, in so many words, right at the start? I did not know, and I was annoyed. But that was not the Invisibles' way of doing things. They never told us until after we had experienced.

Evidently we were supposed—as the cowboys express it—to "roll our own." "There is no substance at all in pure intellect," the Invisibles answered one of my protests. "It is just a very fine shadow. The simplest achievement is so much more important. Pure intellect is aloof, un-related." From her vantage point in the other consciousness Betty ac-cepted this more readily than did I.

"There's such a great difference between your brain and mine," she told me. "Yours is a much better human faculty—so much stronger." But she added, "I can't see why it's so much less absorbent than mine. I don't understand that. It's very puzzling to me—very puzzling. I don't see why brainless instincts like mine are so much easier..." Neither could I. And even the Invisibles refused help.

"They've gone and left me to puzzle this out," said Betty. "I admire brain so much... I don't understand. It looks like some nonconducting quality—a sort of gloss, like glass. There's something..." She broke off for a moment, as if listening.

"Where's the catch? " she ventured.

Again the listening pause.

"Oh, I see! Looks like a ship running with a very strong starboard light and almost no port light. It's a one-eyed thing. It's the other eye they're trying to develop in me." She studied this a few moments.

"I am getting to understand it a little now," she concluded. "The brain looks like a petty officer. Whatever it is incapable of handling it denies. Through generations of denial it has arrested the development of the wiser inner self, which is adapted to handling the higher world of senses and possibilities, the vitalized world around us, what lies out-side human—set limitations. They are not really limitations except as we cramp that inner self." Betty seemed satisfied. I was not. I wanted to see, with the practical eyes of my mind, where I was planting my feet. The Invisibles were patient.

"Make the leap," they urged. "Dare to do it. Take a chance on our being right. You cannot connect up in an unbroken series of steps with what you know. This reality is not on the outskirts; a gap must be bridged.

It is very necessary to employ the measuring stick of your mind ordinarily; but lay it aside intermittently. Hurl yourself into space, as it were. It will not hurt you to go bravely out to pick up a clue or two. You've been trying to creep up on things on the scientific side, but they've got to be boldly taken, artistically, in the present case." "I see what they want! " cried Betty. "Supposing you had to prepare a turtle to become a lark... I'm showing you how to break up the inertia. This leaping, hurling business; this releasing—whatever you want to call it—is definitely the only way to take possession of the wider, freer life." All of which, to me, at that time, tended dangerously near to conventional metaphysical fuzziness; and that was something I did not approve at all. I was very difficult at that period; and if I seem to be doing a lot of talking about myself, it is only because I believe my first view was that of the hard-headed, practical, average man in the street. The phrase "Insult to one's intelligence" occurred to me.

"Don't be offended in your intellect," the Invisibles told me. "Give us a chance. Your precious intellect will have its innings. We won't do more harm than present it something to work on for the rest of its natural life. Leave it in soak and keep it flexible, and we can go on.

It's BOUND to be satisfied later. When this other faculty becomes the leader, your intellect MUST immediately react to it: it MUST, just as the blood goes through your body to nourish all parts. Do you get the idea, now? SOMETHING BEYOND WHAT YOU CAN UNDERSTAND, CAN EXPLAIN WITH THE BRAIN? If that is what we want to get to you first, how COULD we get it through your brain without the slowest of evolution?" As a statement that made sense.

"Please note," they pressed home their point, "you will not get scientific explanation such as you expect. You will get the REALITY as we can manage to give it, which you can deduce as theory later. We cannot tell you in words which would convey anything to you, what we must accomplish by molding you to the thing itself." The molding, it proved, had a definite and ordered method. Betty was much amused at the process.

"It's like children dressing up and playing lady," she commented. "I'm pretending I'm what I'd like to be. It's absurdly dignified." She laughed heartily.

"You ought to see me! It's the way I feel when I wear a train.

It all still looked fuzzy to me, and I said so.

"Couldn't you just take it on faith?" they urged. "Couldn't you just PRETEND for a time, to give it a chance to work? If this reality is ever to be recognized, it must be by something hitherto unrecognized in law.

Put your energy and your daring into throwing out to your farthest limits in search of comprehension of the hitherto unknown. You must GAIN IT IN IMAGINATION FIRST: and then work back through slow steps to connect it with observed facts." And there I was stopped again! By a word! Imagination. I am a fiction writer and I know something about imagination and its power to conjure elaborate structure out of thin air. Also it had kin-folk, such as "wish-fulfillment" and "compensation fantasies." Even Betty was doubtful.

"I don't think," she objected, "that's a very good word—imagination.

It's too cobwebby with unrealities." The Invisibles seemed openly astonished.

"Imagination?" they cried. "Why, that is the very GATEWAY of reality! You call it a plaything. You've always called it a plaything. But actually it's the one thing you possess that connects you with the next substance. It's a transmuting chemical." "It's been the father of a big brood of mistaken ideas," I grumbled.

"Nevertheless," they insisted, "It's the way to get outside yourself.

How else could you function beyond your fleshly limitations? But use imagination masterfully—not as an onlooker: as a partaker.

"The whole trouble," they added, astoundingly, "is in using too little.

A little imagination has no strength to fight. Instead of freeing, it is captured, a poor little helpless thing. A little, taken and concentrated on, shut off from its source of supply, is devitalized, dead.

They had made one convert.

"One must try harder to get hold of the idea and play with it in symbols," agreed Betty enthusiastically. "You've got actually to BE, in imagination, dripping big-leaved plants in the sun against the blue sky.

You've actually got to breathe that idea in before you can make it work, because you are not working in our accustomed substance; you are working in a higher creative form that you don't know how to use, except unconsciously and as it were, relaxed. When you get to a certain age and dignity, you don't play that way. You should. I am not at all impressed by any age or dignity. I am just impressed with actual things and the necessity for them." Whatever my doubts, Betty was completely sold on the idea.

"I want to go on where it is free under the law," she continued. "I want to go on and be more and more the inheritor of these influences. That's it: I want to INHERIT THE LAW. As soon as you become clean-soiled and free-spirited you inherit the law; and that law is a kind of evolution structure. It is what carries you on beyond little man-made experiments.

They are so poky!

# 2.

No discussion of process would be complete were I to omit the exuberant joyousness of the whole performance. This was in no degree damped by the hard and serious work. There was plenty of that, but never did the Invisibles permit it to become portentous or overpowering. Nevertheless it cannot be denied that ordinarily revelation has a certain drag to it.

Saints and Holy Men are proverbially grim and uncompromising. Betty's Invisibles were careful to avoid this. And Betty herself was by nature such a gay and chuckly person that she reacted wholesomely against any inadvertent overstress.

For the idea of asceticism they had nothing but scorn. Giving up a thing—anything—instead of using it in its proper proportion is merely an indication—as Betty herself had always maintained—that you are afraid of it. Funny diets; abstinences of any kind; strict physical regimens—all that sort of thing—were definitely out.

"No negations of any kind interact favorably on the higher centers," said they. "That sounds like a dangerous doctrine, but in reality the danger is more apt to occur on the side of damaging the spontaneity of the body's functions—its buoyancy and equilibrium and youthful confidence and carelessness. Only too easily the aspirations of the inner life misinterpret themselves into such restrictions as an over-regulated child would suffer." Nor would the Invisibles permit either of us to tangle ourselves up in the conventional ideas of "service", "duty", "will-power." "It's not will-power at all! " they protested. "Everything gets so stiff and painful when you do it from the will-power side. Get at it more from the spirit-power, the desire-power side. There's a lift to happiness and harmony which is so much easier than this painful willpower method. This other is like the hard work you do in play. It's glowing, quickening, a life-begetting thing." Betty considered this.

"Work. . .production," she ruminated. "Work is painful; production is better. What can I get that is self-acting? Creation is the nearest to it. That is a cleaner, brighter word. People do not create under a lash." "Above all," said the Invisibles, "don't forget the importance of joyousness through all work. That's the big thing. Think more about that. There is no excuse for dreariness. Dreariness is just contraction." You must never do things MERELY from a sense of duty or "service," said they; you must do them because YOU WANT to do them. And you'll want to do them when you've developed full consciousness! Better not to do them at all otherwise. And, they added astonishingly, YOU CAN GIVE TO OTHERS EFFECTIVELY ONLY FROM OVERFLOW! Duty—and—will-power has no momentum; what they called "automatic-quickening" carries far. And that accompanies only a real desire, and a real enjoyment in the game.

"Keep your attention on savoring, joyously absorbing what you get with the effort," they advised. "So few people are acquisitive enough—so few absorb all they could after they have made the effort. They take only in proportion to what they spend, when there is so much more to be had with a little more effort on the joyous side instead of the struggle side." "Oh! " cried Betty delightedly, "I've been given an attribute of bouncing! We don't any of us bounce high enough—not enough recoil. If we want to be far-flung in happiness, we must think more about the end and less about the effort. We are too near-sighted: we look too much for what is in clear focus. We should look more to the ultimate reward." She checked herself. Then with a comic effort at dignity: "That is a very nice swell idea. It swells me nicely! "The way to free yourself," concluded the Invisibles, "is by EXPANSION OF THE HEART. It is the only possible instrument for shaping your destiny. Without it, the rest is struggle and suffering and delay. With it, all is an open door!"

# 3.

This moving forward blindly in a fog, so to speak, had its clear spots of summary. Every so often, when Betty had advanced to a certain completed phase, she was presented with a blue print of the ground over which she had passed. Sometimes this was cast in a formula, but accompanied always with a warning that it was no hard and fast rule, but only a summary of progress. Here is an example, given in early days—in 1920.

1. The relaxation of the body.
2. The inflowing of the living waters of the spirit.
3. In order not to be swept away by them, the making of "stability," which had been symbolized by Betty as her "shaft." (See *The Betty Book*.)
4. The exertion of will power just to overcome the dead lift; the effort then to climb out; the pushing against the strong current. Then you are ready to start.
5. The putting on of blinders against the earth mind, and thinking with the heart. That is the first outgoing; all the rest has been incoming.
6. The feeling of union with all created things, the expansion sideways supplementing the upward.

At the time this was given, Betty's experiments were still confined to more or less formal sessions under definite control. But now she glimpsed a different possibility.

"That accomplishes a definite something, as a provisional formula," she commented on the above. "However, I think it can be used, not only in this trance state, but in everyday life. It can be used in the life we live, without a bandage over the eyes. It would become then as inspiration, a long breath."

# CHAPTER 11

# LEAVING THE BODY

## 1.

Undoubtedly when entering the higher consciousness, Betty had from the very beginning "left the body", without appreciating the fact. As soon as she realized that she was actually so doing, the Invisibles began to teach her how to do it consciously.

"Escape from the restrictions of the body," said they, "and life outside the restrictions of the body, even while you are occupying it, can be experienced. That is the real life. How can any sensible person doubt it? We are trying to shatter the bodily conception of life in order to expose the other to view. The discovery of this other conception and the gradual acquisition of it is what constitutes the RAISON D'ETRE of your existence. If you do not discover it, you have failed; you are either standing still or slipping back." Most of the training to accomplish this was technical, intended for Betty individually, and in no sense to be taken as general instruction.

It was only one of the necessary means to an end. So I quote bits here and there from the record merely to give a picture of the sort of thing that went on.[12] "I see! " said Betty, in running comment. "Now!

---

[12] Condensed version used in *Across The Unknown*.

just to slip off my body. . .leave it lying on the floor. . .so much easier to work from this end back... I'm getting so much more at home here." An interval followed, with no comment.

"Now they've brought me back to contemplate my body. They think I can improve my control..." Again the pause.

"They're just letting me into my body and out again—just a flash, to get control of doing it... It's wonderful practise in a kind of balance—in keeping my spirit so balanced that it gets no drag from the body... I've got to keep quiet to do this, or I'll never get anywhere... This is fine! So much more strength this way! See how much quieter I am lying." "Practise in leaving the body," said the Invisibles to me by way of explanation. Then in command to Betty: "Enter the body... Now release." "I've got to keep leaving and entering, alternating," said Betty.

Short silence.

"My head and neck are tired in my body," she complained presently. "I'd like to turn... I'm going to try... So painful to think about my body." She tried to move, but failed.

"Shall I move your head for you?" I asked.

"Toward the wall," said Betty.

I obeyed.

"That's better." There ensued a long silence—but obviously a busy silence.

"I can't hold it any more," said she at last. "I fell over. I oughtn't to have done that. Now I can rest, they say.

Here ensued another long silence, but this time obviously not busy.

"Try once more," the Invisibles told her at last.

Another pause.

"Yes, I can do it!" said Betty. "Now wait until I alternate again...

I did it! That's very, very useful." The "lesson" continued thus for upward of an hour. Then Betty was free to tell me a little something about it—while still in her trance state.

"You withdrew all attention from your body, which is very difficult," she told me. "I thought of it as so heavy as to be impossible to move; while I, the living, left it in the comer and walked off in my spiritual body. That worked until my hay fever wanted to make me sneeze.

"The main thing is that, during the day, about your affairs, you can at odd moments, practice retiring to that spiritual body. Withdraw attention from the other, until you get helpful control. It is very important for me to learn it...

"I'm going to come out pretty soon: I'm just hanging around...

"It is a matter of withdrawing attention from one thing, and giving it full strength to another. It must be done before I can go on. They can't keep on dragging my body around. I've got to get control so I can leave that entirely behind. They say the reason I always come back so soon is that I'm a self-stopper. I've got to stop wobbling and prepare to go all the way and not want to snap back. It is like standing on my head. It's that 'Oh dear, I'm going to wobble and come down' idea that brings me back." "The more you can relax the body all the time," said the Invisibles, "the more power you possess and the more you can use the spiritual in contact with the physical. Ignore the body, except for its necessary functions. The first point is to keep it in health, so that it can be the more easily ignored." "Now I am going to do it over again," said Betty. "This must be made more trustworthy... Such a strange light..." For some little time she was silent.

"I can travel a little now," she resumed. "Getting the idea of unattached motion. I've been so tethered before. But it is hard for me to see; it's so dim." "One of the most powerful forces is belief in your power to do it," said the Invisibles. "That combined with effort to make good in it, will accomplish almost anything. Without that you sink into your own limitations and consider them impossible to overcome. But if you get the belief that it can be done and back it up: presto! It is done, and you have opened new doors. It is the haleness of trying doggedly without the belief that gets you nowhere." "I've always wanted to explain that holding-steady process that gets you here, but I've never been able to," said Betty. "I think I'd call it a condensation of purpose; but condensation is not quite it, because it depends so much on expansion and breadth of perception."

## 2.

With practise, "getting out of the body," like the other things, became for Betty less and less a question of concentration and struggle. One day—after several months of off—and—on practice—she suddenly seemed to understand the knack.

"Why! " she cried, somewhat astonished, "I can slip back and forth easily today! It is very strange! The wind swept through me as I came in. I hailed it, did not crouch before it, and it went through me as sun goes through you. I wasn't conscious of my body any more; I was just conscious of vigorous well-being almost as disembodied as one could

hope to be. Harmonious vitality superseded the mortal sensation."
She paused in her reporting, apparently trying out her newfound skill.

"I like slipping back and forth that way," she confided presently. "I don't see why it isn't just as interesting a performance, and vastly more desirable, as learning to swim in an element that is not your own.

It is Just as natural, really. I just leap out of myself, and take a dive into a freer and more stimulating element. Each time I do it, it gets easier; I am more at home in it; and more stimulated by it. I am not tremendously good at it; but it's just as simple as that."

# 3.

From then on Betty had little or no trouble with the "getting out" part, but the return to the body without undesirable repercussion, so to speak, was another matter.

"The danger of this experience is always in coming back," she explained to me, "in arousing the body, like an invalid who thinks she's been abused... That's the attitude with which you must look at your bodily weaknesses always. You must be their trained nurse, giving them only such attention as is wholesome and such care as is necessary and such sympathy as is good for them...

She broke off to consider this.

"And," she continued, "there's no use saying:, 'I'll do it next time.' Not next time: this time. 'This is the only time there is,'—you must say that to yourself.

You are not rising above the body, after the usual method; you're non-existing it, humorously, ridiculing it out of its habits. But, after all, one's so likely to be more in the frame of mind of the family relative than of the trained nurse." "Listen," said the Invisibles. "There is a kind of invalid's room in which your body has established its habits and weaknesses. You are coming back now, but you are not going to let your active, vigorous, pulsing, living being more than visit and cheer that room." "Well," said Betty, "I'll just stay quiet and pack up my ideas... I must come away. I'm getting drowsy, and I am a little afraid of that state in between, but I have to pass through it each time.

"I'm coming back." A pause. "I'm almost back... It seems like a fairy-story world now."

# CHAPTER 12

# REST ON ATTAINMENT

## 1.

All of Betty's instructions, and all of the work she was called upon to do, conformed to the law of rhythm. That is to say, she had alternate periods of activity and of rest. But the usual notion of rest as semi-comatose loafing was promptly knocked from under us. After a prolonged period of what she termed "striving," Betty considered herself entitled to what she called a "sag-back" party.

"The way you sag back when boresome callers go at last," she explained.

And at once she made an astounding discovery.

"Why!" she cried, "that's funny! It certainly is! I hunted and hunted, and there is not any place in the whole universe where you can slump!—I fell behind looking for it. Now somebody's helping me catch up just to see what it feels like, the difference. No place to slump! Not even when you catch up! It is less strain to keep your place, it's a more comfortable feeling there's no standing still—You can stand still, if you want to," she decided after further investigation, "but you can't sit down." This paradox puzzled her. She retired into another of those inner experiences of hers which I always hoped was going to mean something or other to me—in time.

"They straightened me out in fine shape," she confided presently. "I had lost my equilibrium and sat down. It's a funny thing, but you can't do that; you've got to keep going when you once start. It's as if you were to decide that your heart had beat long enough, and you thought you'd stop it a while." It was only later, and after several sessions of gropings, that she again reported anything to me.

"After every great spiritual effort I've always been left with a slightly vacuum-like spent feeling," said she. "As if I'd put in my all and was entitled to a vacation, a slight reaction, a slump,—getting back to a comfortable and ordinary level. That's the way I've been doing, the way everybody does. Well now, there's another kind of relaxation, another kind of rest. Instead of going back each time to your own starting place, which is merely an unnecessary habit, discard that idea, and enjoy resting on the... She stumbled for a word or phrase.

"Rest on attainment," supplied the Invisibles, cryptically.

Here was a new concept for Betty to absorb and to clarify.

## 2.

"The only relaxation is in accustomedness," the Invisibles tried to explain. "When you get accustomed to a thing it does not tire you; you can rest in your attainment. You may just as well give up right now any idea of slumping, because you never can, unless you back out. All you can do is to work so hard you get used to it, so that it doesn't tire you. There's great joy in it, though, when you get there." It did not sound very restful to me. I said so.[13]

"They say I mustn't think of being wracked and spent and tired," said Betty. "I must rest in what I have attained. That is the real refreshment. It doesn't tire you so much when you start expanding if you rest on

---

[13] "But you missed the point," Joan writes me, in comment on this part of the MS. "Of course you 'rest on attainment'! Take mere physical dexterity, like learning to knit, which I did not do until about five years ago. My fingers were stiff and clumsy; I lost stitches off my needle; it was very hard for this old dog to learn new tricks. I was about to give up in despair. Then suddenly I could knit! Now when I am weary I rest myself by knitting. Work one knows how to do is never wearying when pursued normally. We rest on that attainment, and only tire over some new process of learning. Transfer this fact from the physical into Betty's spiritual, and you'll understand." I think Joan is right.

what you've attained. That's quite nice! It transfers your center of consciousness. Such a new way of resting!" With an air of discovery she announced that this feeling-tired-business is largely a matter of what the body seems to expect of us.

"I am apt to think I am tired when I come back," said she, "but it's only a peevish kind of resentment of my body. I'll just ignore that. I'm not tired: I'm just USED,—like a slate. I can brush it off and fix it.

"I must never," she continued, "admit a weak or tired thought at that stage. If I do, it dilutes the impression; like leaving something unstoppered. It runs out." "Stay up on your hilltop; make yourself at home there," advised the Invisibles. "No sense in you—the real you—coming back. Rest up there and have a new starting point. This going back every time is just poor technique. You can do it, but it's clumsy and laborious." "It's nice to stay up," admitted Betty, after she had considered this, "but it's new-nice. I still want to go back and slump; that's old-nice.—Well, I'll try it— "It's a stronger kind of rest," she reported to me. "Sort of leaving your consciousness on the top shelf instead of bringing it back to rest on unpadded nerves." She was silent so long that I asked her what she was doing. "I'm tidying up to come back," said she.

# 3.

"Now listen," said the Invisibles, "there's no restless feeling of perpetual motion about it. It's more a feeling of warm existence, like quiet and very active rays. It's like the sun growing things—that kind of life. It keeps you living outside, in advance of yourself, instead of occupied with your physical self." "I'll try it," agreed Betty, "I won't allow myself to THINK when I'm tired. When I'm tired I'll be in a derrick and lift automatically without thinking. It will probably work, if you say so." She sounded doubtful. "I see—it will be outside of MYSELF. It'll take some doing! " She chuckled. "Me a derrick! Make it mechanical. I see: instead of damaging my real substance by drawing on it. All right; come on, we'll go try it." "Don't spend YOURSELF on what your mechanism can do," supplemented the Invisibles.

"I know lots of things but I can't teach myself them," observed Betty quaintly, "I want to go now with myself that knows lots of things. It's nice not to try to understand, just to know." Ensued a long pause. "I did not come all the way back!" she cried triumphantly, "I DISTINCTLY did not come all the way back today. I may not be able to stay there—"

"The main thing is not to slump back automatically. You can be at ease without being out of formation," said the Invisibles.

"What was that expression?" queried Betty. "Rest in attainment. At first I thought that a terrible idea. But there is rest to it. Only, I don't get it unless I've attained. It's the rest you find in being, unconscious of your struggle because you are strong enough for it." Apparently she eventually surrounded the technique to her own and the Invisibles' satisfaction. Years later she had this to say: "It used to be such an effort to keep going: now it's such a discomfort to stop. My being seems to consist entirely of the feeling of a machine in action. I'm set in action; wound up; my machinery is going. It's the feeling of the next stratum of energy above us which they talked about." There is indeed, said she, a rhythm of rest and accomplishment. It is the rest of incoming and outgoing.

"I wish I could find a name for it all. There is a poised well-being about this thing. It is a vigorous rest. I'm enthusiastic and vigorous; yet I'm resting—without slumping. How would I say that? Rest isn't the word: it's a pause of consciousness. It's a kind of radiation, which is a sort of worship. There ought to be some name for that pause in application that sort of shoots out. It ought to be done lots, to fill up the gaps, to heal. Lots of it is needed everywhere, all through life; it's a kind of ventilation. I'll just do it a while and see if some word comes up to claim it." But no word did.

# CHAPTER 13

# THE NEAR COUNTRY

When Betty first set out on her Road, it seemed to her—and hence to me—that she journeyed far to touch even the first contact with these new and strange "forces". And when she came actually to that phase in which she "left the body" in order to explore or to follow wheresoever in the "other consciousness" she was led, the impression of distance was deepened. She so expressed her experience.—"I'm going away off now." "My! I'm going deep!. . . Still farther?" "I'm being taken away now." Always the impression of TRAVEL to some remote destination. And when she faced back the return trip seemed to her as long.

This impression, astoundingly, proved to be an illusion. It arose, I think, partly from Betty's own sense of radical CHANGE of environment, which in our world ordinarily means distance; and partly from mankind's age-long mental habit of considering heaven "up" and hell "down," and the heavenly messengers descending to us on ladders or beams of light.

After Betty had gone to her Unobstructed Universe, she showed an amusing impatience over this idea. She was talking, through Joan, to a young woman she had known well in our life. Something was said that indicated confusion in the latter's mind. Betty stopped the discussion with the abrupt question: "What is your idea of where I am now, anyway? "Why," replied the young woman, rather vaguely, " why, I just think of you as suspended somehow, in space." "I AM RIGHT HERE!" stated Betty vigorously. "There is only one universe.

There is no separate 'heaven.' My world is your world plus."[14] Even while here, she grew to understand that the two phrases, "leaving the body" and "going far", were only a manner of speaking, and that she could modify them to advantage. Leaving the body became more a matter of withdrawing—completely—ATTENTION from the body. And the "journey" simply did not exist! "It makes the world seem so small," she commented, " when you reach out for people, and the space between somehow shuts up like a telescope. I don't understand that. Got to do some experimenting around. I don't see how you can pull out and push in space like that..." The following long pause was obviously occupied in the "experimenting around." "Why, how astonishingly near that brings things!" she burst out. "Isn't that astonishing! Why, ISN'T that astonishing! Even the distance to the other consciousness is not a distance of space; it's a slowness or torpidity in penetrating. It's just lack of the right combination that makes it seem distant. It is so near when you clear that intervening denseness which is not space...

"How can I tell this? Supposing I was in a dark room, and then a bright light was turned on. The darkness and the light occupy the same area, don't they? One overcomes the other and reveals what the other did not.

Well, instead of being in the dark substance of consciousness, I'm in the brighter revealing one. Density is gone. I'm in the same place I was, but with greater vision.

"It is all one; here; now. All the heavens and bells and universes superimposed. Why, that is perfectly tremendous! It gets nearer and nearer until it all seems right on top of me! More and more revealing light! . . .

"I can't pierce it further. I'm not big enough: it would overwhelm me and burst me. I can't do it...

This was enormously interesting to me at the time. It is more so today, for now it appears as the first inkling of the brilliant exposition of Space and Time Betty was to give us, fifteen years later through Joan, in her book, *The Unobstructed Universe*.

In the immediately subsequent sessions the concept was further developed.

"I see!" she began, after a long interval of silent investigation, "space is only an imaginary boundary, not a definite reality. How curious it

---

[14] I quoted this incident in *The Unobstructed Universe*, but it is worth repetition here.

looks! There isn't any such thing as that word-pattern we call space. It's altogether different! . .

She paused to examine further.

"This is too much for me! " she resumed. "My goodness! There's no use trying to figure it out while you're living. You couldn't hold on to the idea when you brought it back! I don't believe I could STAND an idea like that and get back and live again sensibly. But I'll try to tell you. I'm gasping over it, and I'll spoil it; but I'll try— "Yesterday when I looked at a pebble under the microscope, I looked down into a deep canon of space. I can walk on that pebble; and yet, by the magic of concentration, a tiny crevice in it can be refracted to the illusion of a real canon with true immensity. How can you measure space? How can you give anything so elastic and changing the name of space? Don't you see, space is not real at all. It is contained in an attribute of your consciousness." "Consider," suggested the Invisibles, "the magnitude of your own illusion of space as compared with the space of an unperfected pebble.

Now raise it again to an incomprehensible magnitude such as you can only guess at." Betty thought this over awhile. Then, in a puzzled tone: "We are all apparently occupying the same space. It doesn't seem to be a case of distance at all... This is quite new to me and very satisfactory; because I never could see how they'd have room for everything and everybody who'd ever died. This is much better; only I can't understand it clearly...

"Well, anyhow, I'm never going to have any respect for space again, because I know now it's altogether too unreliable. It depends utterly on who is looking at it. I'm sorry I did not get that intelligently, but anyway it was a grand muckraking and exposure of space! You see, it's a word that hasn't any standing at all, except with us. It represents only what we think about it. But I must say it's rather exhausting to struggle with, since I don't seem to have much influence with it, and yet have work to do in it!" "Space is not distance," concluded the Invisibles. "Space is degrees of perception. Distance is only slowness in getting there." "How can one speak of 'life beyond'," cried Betty, "when THERE is HERE!"

# CHAPTER 14

# GATES BEYOND GATES

## 1.

That concept—the HERENESS rather than the THERENESS—had at least the merit of relieving my own mind. I had never quite liked the idea that Betty was being taught to "leave her body" and go sky-hooting off into unknown and distant spaces. But if leaving the body meant, as it now seemed, merely a complete withdrawal of attention from the body, and a transfer of being into a different center of the same consciousness, why then that wasn't so bad. Nevertheless the new field was "remote" in that, without such training as Betty was receiving, we enter it consciously only through the portals of death.

In that sense, at least, she was exploring a distant world. Exploration of this new region was not merely to satisfy curiosity: it had a definite purpose, concerned as it was with universals.

"I am always afraid of being monkey-minded over here," she told me.

"There's so much to see and do." Though the Invisibles described the purpose as "expansion of consciousness," that appeared to have a number of facets. She was to learn wisdom by precept and actual experience: she was to establish headquarters in the higher consciousness from which to direct her daily life: she was even to develop certain supernormal powers which are generally lumped under the term "occult."

This last was an alluring sideline. It had the fascination of taking rabbits out of hats. Doubtless that is why it is made the end and aim of many so-called systems of development. The average of us, whether we believe or wholly scoff, like to bear about Adepts and Masters and White and Black Magicians and Witch Doctors and Voodoo, but only as they are able to perform mystifying stunts. Well, in due time Betty learned to perform stunts, when they were useful to the main objective—but only THEN.

That was the point. Either she or the Invisibles—I forget which—once stated the criterion for that sort of thing. "When a means is made an end-in-itself, it at once becomes a deterrent." In other words, conscious attempts to develop psychic powers for their own sakes are putting the cart before the horse, and are quite likely dangerous in the long run. The safe road is to seek higher consciousness, and then such psychic powers as are useful to that end accompany, or follow as a by-product. Betty DID acquire psychic powers. But she was never much interested in them, except as faculties to be utilized in the world of higher consciousness as we utilize our faculties of sight and hearing in our own world.

Nevertheless, as they were her faculties and for her use, enough legitimate occasion in ordinary life happened by to furnish material for many chapters of the believe-it-or-not variety, were the telling of such our program. For instance, as we have seen, she had been taught very definitely how to leave her body, in the occult sense. But that ability was for the purpose of her explorations, and she confined her use of it to just that purpose, except on a few rare and obviously legitimate occasions. As when she reached across the continent three thousand miles to the sick-room of a relative. She reported to me how he was, she described the room, who was in that room, and what they were doing; details confirmed to the last item by letter.

She also learned to partake of another's mind which is perhaps more accurate than saying she could " read" another's thoughts; and—again on very rare occasions—did so; but ordinarily her scruples would not permit.

"It would be an invasion of privacy," said she.

Doing psychic work in the usual sense for others was no part of her job; and this aspect, too, she declined. However, because the circumstances made it seem to her almost obligatory, she solved a mystery as to whether murder or suicide, so convincingly that not only did the widow receive a large sum of insurance, but a rascally business associate was glad to disgorge.

Over the period of years such things happened—not often—but when they did they were of practical value.

# 2.

For most of us, I think, such unique possibilities would have held something of a lure. But Betty was not much tempted. Her interest was too completely centered in the exploration of her new world. And this, even I could see, was a man-sized job.

Betty's attempts to describe that world were a constant struggle. This new region, it seemed, was so utterly novel as to be next to inexpressible. But apparently the reporting back was an essential part of her program, perhaps for crystallization in her own mind, perhaps for my benefit.

"I am trying hard to accustom myself, because I dimly feel I must acquire for you an actual knowledge of these fundamentals," she told me.

"They must be made living, vibrating intensifications of your consciousness, not just dead symbols of vaguely comprehended verities. I must accomplish it, first in my own exploratory fashion, then in its refinements and adaptations—its mental concepts and its verbal monuments." Naturally she had a human desire to share her discoveries.

"I take such a childish delight in having a private world," she confided. "I'm so bursting with it sometimes that it seems as though people must know I have a big secret... I'll make a beautiful window so they can look and see what I see." This was ordinarily her attitude. But once in a while she balked a little at marring the clarity of her vision by any attempt at translation.

"Oh, but it would spoil it so to make a diagram of it!" she protested.

"It's such a fragile thing! It's just begun... Please! Have I got to spoil it?" She seemed to listen; then added in a confidential whisper: "Let's put it away quietly, as it is; just tiptoe away and leave it, like the bird's nest I used to visit." Again she paused. To me it was like listening to one end of a telephone conversation.

"I don't think I can say it," she yielded at last. "I'll try.

"It is like living on the edge of a vast forest," she began. "I've lived in a clearing all my life. Now I'm going to slip into the forest. It's full of wonderful things, and I've got to find my way through. . .

She fell silent.

"I'm getting the fullness of it now," she went on presently. "It's a beautiful rest hall of the spirit. I can't describe it, but it offers marvelous strengthening peace. If I could only establish this in the midst of world affairs, it would make a proper domicile in which to produce power and equipment for competent work..." She paused again, as if in contemplation.

"I feel so strongly this great vaulted life of limitless health, vitality and possibility, surging, pulsing with power and rhythm...

Resonance—it has a beautiful sound, made up of the harmony of little voices, like the pulse of a summer night. It is so alive this vaulted life. It is all feel and happiness. How can I describe it? It has a richness we know nothing about all the tones of youth combined with all the depth of maturity. And there's such abounding energy to it—such abounding joy! In it I feel as if in perfect physical health. My body actually radiates—there's an outgoing of something which manufactures harmony. I don't know what the substance of it is, but it resembles intense appreciation. I wish there were a name for it. If I said 'worship' it would mean something else to most people. We have nothing like it. The warmest human glow you can imagine—affection, sympathy— cannot approach it in intensity. They are just sparks from it.

. . ." She sighed deeply.

"I am hunting, hunting for recognized words and terms for this feeling of abounding life. I can't find anything but the word enthusiasm. That's the liveliest little word I can find. All the rest are torpid. It is discouraging to hunt and hunt around among all these logical and legal and leveling things and not find flame-leaping words. It's too bad! For some moments she was still.

"My world! " she continued, with something like reverence. "The intensity of it is almost like suffering, it is so acute. I am roaming, almost despairing, hunting for terms. It is life at the meridian—it casts no shadow. It is life at its core. To translate it would wrench me to pieces. I must keep quiet..." As a dealer in words I thought she was doing very well, and I said so.

But she was dissatisfied. To her the thing itself was so much more vivid than any possible reflection of it.

"To try to tell of it," she disagreed tersely, "is like trying to bottle sunshine. In ordinary terms it simply does not convey itself."

# 3.

To the very end Betty continued to find the higher consciousness largely untranslatable. Necessarily, therefore, she often resorted to symbolism.

Much of this was arresting and beautiful. I cannot here quote adequately.[15] But the following will serve as an example: "I've entered the hinterland of consciousness," said Betty. "Everything is radiance-filled and fresh and eager-spirited, as on a pinnacle day of extreme youth and extreme tiptoeness for life, more life..." She broke off, leaving me to wonder what was going on.

"I'm playing a most amusing game," she explained presently. "I'm busy collecting different phases of the spell of this country. It is not a tellable thing, but I'll see what is obtainable in word patterns...

"All the words are too pompous," she continued. "They are too ponderous for the playful, blissful thing I'm doing. It is like the great, booming comfort of being in the water. I lie on my back in the embrace of the water, only conscious of its caress when I move. It so perfectly surrounds and accepts and sports with me. I tear it up; I tear the water up to see it mend itself so derisively, just laughing its bubbles at the futility of my efforts. I am stroking the water as I swim in the sense of its soft encompassing, and piercing it with arms thrust out. Broken drops flash back...

"I wonder if I could collect in words some of the sun spell too? I want to get the different phases in fragments, and then bring them together for that spell of enchantment which is the hinterland of consciousness.

"Now, the sun! It is very commanding. It is not so playful. All I do is to lie subordinate to it. It takes possession of me. Without resistance I give up to its expansion. Magically it dispels my clothes and enters into my bones. My very skeleton grows larger and lighter under its influence. My mind is lulled. I am all atoms and chemistry, all separated and spread out. I might be a mere heat radiation for all the tangibility there is of me...

"It's too bad I don't understand music, for it is all around me all the time. I get into the sweep of it, into the control and abandon of what you might call great engulfing cadences, which absorb discord and turn it into harmony. It is a curious kind of music—an intoxicating rhythm of things. If you get tired you just let go, and it sweeps you along and rests you...

---

[15]   There is much of it in *Across The Unknown*.

"There's always a strong temptation to abandon myself completely—and yet I never do. I always want to; and I always put it deliberately aside as dangerous. I wonder why! It is curiously like fighting off drowsiness.

There is always the instinct to concentrate on something practical...

"I think perhaps there's danger of getting drowned, of getting unbalanced and losing your perception. There comes a woozy point, a giving way to the drunk sensation. That's the danger point...

"I wonder what those body strings are that can be strained only so much at a time. As I come back I realize somebody has watched over them."

# 4.

For a long time I was certainly no help to Betty in her struggle for expression. I was still looking for something "definite." I think my effort to pin things down put her on the defensive. The Invisibles did their best to combat this attitude. They were always encouraging her to loosen up; to make an amusing game of it.

They tell me it is just play." Betty herself was speaking. "They only want to make it play. It keeps the right balance...

"Oh dear!" she begged. "I want to get it into something tangible for Stewart. You've got to cast a material shadow for him. You've got to make it into something like coin he can spend to get things with, or he won't think it any good!" She paused a moment.

"I feel as though I had dived to a great depth to get something for you," she told me, "and when I came up and looked at it with your eyes, it was nothing but a cockleshell." As I look back I realize I must have been a great trial, nevertheless I believe my insistences were useful. My stubbornness gave Betty an anchor to windward; counteracted any danger of drifting. At least the Invisibles were kind enough to tell me so.

Betty realized that for this period anyway, we must have different points of view.

"I am emboldening myself," she told me one day, after a long initial pause, "and it takes time. Funny game!. . . I have to embolden myself in order to acquire an authoritative presentation of things. You see, we work in different mediums. Yours offers adjustment to the highest reaches of comprehension compatible with earth conditions; my records are translations from other conditions extending beyond normal experience. Each time I have to transmute myself for participation to the best of my ability in the new conditions, and then struggle to turn them into word symbols giving approximate concepts. I keep my contacts with you by passing back and forth from one type of comprehension to the other. It is slow hard work, but it has to be done. I hold my little bit of consciousness as on a magic carpet, miraculously freed from what I can only symbolize to you as terrestrial gravitation—that being the hampering customary conditions as compared with this greater scope of action...

"Coming here is like coming from a stingy little cabin to magically wrought palaces and vaulted temples, with still more beautiful places beyond—a vast and colorful world purpled over with mystic promises. How can I tell you these things, when they are so big and I am so little? My audacity in even sensing them awes me!. . .

"Today's experience seems to be a lesson in selection. There appears to be an elaboration and richness in my surroundings which surpasses all my powers of perception. I sense intricacies of beauty I cannot even comprehend. I could easily lose myself in convolutions of the varied appeals to my senses.

"Fortunately there is within me a controlling desire and ability to see a few great simplicities of this different and more powerfully vital form of life. While I can sense the stupendously manifold lesser manifestations existing in this particular arc of my illumination, at the same time I can see the fundamental motivations behind them. Because of my hold on these I can support the wealth and beauty and elaboration.

"My effort," she interrupted herself to explain, "is always and always will be, to do the thing itself before I can know about it."

# 5.

Obviously many of Betty's experiences were symbolic shows arranged by the Invisibles. For example: "I am carefully approaching something—a great Presence." It was Betty speaking. "I want to see if I can make out who he is and what he has to tell me...

"Now I can't come any nearer to him, so I will just have to listen carefully. Something is shaping vaguely, as a mass comes to form on a potter's wheel...

"He is showing me carefully guarded treasures. I know they are treasures, but I don't know what to value them with. I am to select from them as the natural appeal is to me. And then I am to wear them, because of the dignity and responsibility they imply, as a treasure bearer should. It is like an emblem of office laid on me, and I am trying to conduct myself as worthy. I wish you could understand what this kind of spiritual pride is, how it differs from the pride of arrogance. It is a lofty tingling thing that is married to humility.

"It must be a great poverty of spirit that makes people go unadorned with the emblems of their belief. These emblems now being showed me are beautiful things, so marvelous in design and workmanship, so distinguished in prerogative. They mark the rank that serves. They acknowledge before all men's eyes the grandeur of kinship, the unity of human experiences. I go appareled thus in crowded places, a member of a great fraternity, seen of all men, but unrecognized by the saddening majority. I am not at all self-conscious about these things I wear, because mockers do not seem to notice them—at least they do not believe they are real...

"I could not pick out much of that treasure: I did not dare. I had only courage enough to see about two things I could support. I took a beautiful golden disc thing to wear over my heart to keep it from hardening, to keep it tender in spite of contacts with the world. I wanted that very much, very much. And then there was a banner I wanted to hold up over the crowd where all people could see it; but I did not take that because my hands would not be free, and I must have freed hands. The thing I did take was a kind of cloak. It had only a back to it. Somehow it keeps me going forward. I couldn't turn around and go back in it. I do not care much about the backward—looking part of me, and I wanted to cover it up with something that was more nearly the texture of my ideal.

"There are so many things in that treasure heap. I just selected the things that would give me strength.

There is a mass of beauty in them, so curiously wrought with every human perception and precious instinct. There is a long golden chain I would like to have had. It was a chain of concentration that does not bind, does not restrain you from expanding; but I did not take it. I wanted it, too; but I did not think I was fit to wear it yet. It is a great pity, because everybody who knows anything will notice that something is lacking. I'll go back some day and get it,"

# 6.

"I feel it just as a vast current! " Betty was trying to describe another aspect of her 'private world.' "I am in connection with that current. Little nerve-scattering things cannot hurt me. But that's not enough. How can I arrest and deflect it, this mighty force? How can I handle it? It sweeps through and by me, partaking of me. How can I partake of it? Suppose you found yourself in a mighty thing like this; what would you do? I've got to decide." She studied the problem.

"When you come over here," she continued, "this force is all you've got to begin your work with. All you have is the amount you can take and arrange. I take stock of myself—sense how much individualized current is around me which keeps at bay, as it were, what would be an all-engulfing substance if I'd let it. But I'm not going to let it engulf me, I'm going to act on it. That is as near as I can get to sensation, the first primitive sensation of creative force which I manufacture and maintain.

"It is the growth of this sensation of greater and greater radius of superior force acting on the primal substance which will make it possible for me to establish my ideal, what I actually am capable of, what my SPECIES is in the universal plan. I said species because my ideal, my little atomic arrangement I am capable of making, establishes my species in the universe. And I am capable of changing it continually.

"This makes the whole universe dependent on the amount of the life force one is able to generate and utilize. One's participation in the abounding beauty of the whole Plan is dependent only on one's own efforts. One is tremendously responsible for one's radius. That is what one is judged by." She broke off.

"I am making it very difficult and unattractive today, I am afraid," she apologized, "because it is the beginning of an aspect very hard to put into words. But later the avidity and desire come which lift me into the case of it, like laughing, or breathing in the spring air, or anything else that is the gift of life...

"I feel as if I had stepped all over a bed of flowers telling you about it." Again, at another time, another attack from another angle: "I am," she said, "very busy getting a consciousness of my aliveness for you to put down later. It's an acknowledgment and exercise of acute aliveness. I must prepare it first in quiet. It is one of the secrets of all inner creative work and progress and self-propulsion...

"One of the most essential motivations of progress," put in the Invisibles, "is the reality of this very thing, this acute aliveness, this warm eager current ever seeking new channels. Without a definitely encouraged consciousness of this aliveness you are not yet in possession of your highest capabilities. But when you gain it for your own, you will have forever in your hands the magic open—sesame of gates beyond gates. You cannot realize all the difference between what has always existed as the common eternal history of the race, and the few inheritors of actual treasure. The astonishing power, the intense stimulation beyond anything you can conceive intellectually, is the reward that awaits your efforts.

"You grasp intellectually what the raising of vibrations means. Yet could you, deliberately, sitting in your chair, raise your vibrations; and, clearly aware of the act, describe and control the accompanying emotion? This is, quite simply, the trained approach to acute aliveness." "I cannot accomplish it through the channel of my mind," Betty took it up. "I must experiment and tell you myself...

"I can, for instance, walk from here to the door in various degrees of vibration—which I call that for lack of a better term. I can go as a human lima bean, for instance: life contained within an ungerminated shell, you know. I can walk somewhat in that fashion without particular sense impressions on the way. Or I can go with perhaps some simple idea occupying me, of some business or pleasure. Or I can go in various degrees above that, admitting more and more of life to my inner being, in proportion as I am increasingly released from my restricting shell.

Or, finally, I can go with acute aliveness, which is the master dispeller of that containing shell; so that, while I walk seemingly as before, utilizing the same functions, actually I am permitting a flooding—in of the greater all-encompassing self. I would then walk towards the door in a beautiful spare moment, occupied happily and naturally in merging myself. There's the secret. Like warm sun rays on a gratefully receptive body, in the pregnant moment of eternity in passing to the door, all the richness of life would flood through me; and I, comfortably, deeply happy in my, merging with it, would slowly learn the secret of acute awareness and all that it horizons to my soul.

"I can't tell you what it really feels like: words don't hold it nicely.

But it's not only a flooding-in, there's an ebb to it, and you flood out with it. Nevertheless I do not, somehow, lose control of my segment of life. The participation temporarily in the greater unity just expands the segment." "The great effort being made today," concluded the Invisibles, "is to impart the gift of knowledge of the true nature of spiritual practises.

It has been so unhumanized, so undesirably presented, so scoffed at and misunderstood. The time is ripe to present it as a warmth and shelter and beauty of the inner life, as ardently to be desired and worked for as those of the outer."

# CHAPTER 15

# INVISIBLE ALLIANCES

## 1.

"This is difficult," was Betty's rather puzzled comment one day. "No more inspiration poured in. I am up against a curious kind of waiting for some acts of mine. I see that clearly, but can't seem to make the effort.

"I feel as if my hands and feet were bound," said she, "and yet I was told to make my first experiment "At first I fussed and objected at being thrust so soon, so unprepared, as it were, into the stream of workers in spiritual force. But then I realized I was accompanied by something I was sure eventually to attain...

"I went back to my hook-up with the Source to see what first clumsy thing I would do to utilize my power," said she. "The first thing I wanted was affiliation, a heart affiliation that abolished separateness. That makes for strength. The second thing I wanted was to make an impress of my convictions. It did not have to be noisy or clamorous, but it did have to be steady and motivating. How few make impressions: only the quiet and the martyred." She was supposed to do something. What? "Naturally I was much at a loss, but I did do some thing. Do you want to know what I did? It is a sort of foolish thing to tell; but the first thing I did was to throw out all the warmth and happiness

I could collect and hurl forth. I decided I was going to have my own circumambience that everybody would like to come into. It would be like a glowing river in its unimpeded progress, with song on the way, and sparkle—And, by Jove, I was going to see that it kept up its exuberance and dance and vitality and fling! I got enthusiastic about it, and I worked terribly hard, until I found out, after I had made it, that I carried myself along quite gaily." This met with approval, as a beginning.

"You realize how useless and futile you are; you try hard and experiment until you acquire something with which to work," said the Invisibles.

"This," said Betty with satisfaction, apparently describing the state of consciousness to which this brought her, "seems to be ahead in productivity of any other surroundings I've had. It is a place where things are done, and done efficiently. I've got all the release and freedom of striding on hilltops and through spring-swept days, and the feeling of superlative powers within." Apparently the method of the moment was to throw her overboard, as one teaches a puppy to swim.

"I am," said she after a long silence, "plopped out into a place of turmoil and stress beating upon my serenity. It was like a fire drill, a first aid course, what to do in an emergency. I remembered the advice given for the physical zero hours. Leave pain and puzzlement outside, they said, and creep to your quiet center. Let your heart seek close proximity to the divine spark, believing in its power to remagnetize you. Be still. Let it work." "This," interjected the Invisible, "is the same thing as what we have called taking directly from the Source. It supplies harmony fitted and prepared for instantaneous use, with all the warmth necessary for the continued life of that harmony in practical affairs." "The chaotic din and discord continued around me," Betty went on, "and I thought, 'I must fly to my army of invisible friends. With them I must hastily fling out worship, thankfulness for knowledge of superior weapons, claiming the reinforcement of them, determined that the constructive forces would inform my action.' Then I stepped out naturally into the battle, and held on to my determination, and let it work. A great pressure came against me, like the swift currents we could barely stand against in crossing the Alaskan rivers. A great pressure was on me, and I felt my inadequacy: It was an emergency. What could I do to maintain myself, and to act against the current, as it were, like a power-ship against the tides? At once I reinforced myself with the strength of the army of invisible friends we have been unifying. The pressure was still there, but the crisis had passed, turned by superior strength.

"You see, our best weapons are really our invisible alliances. That part must not be neglected, as it is our present field of action. Action without the directing power of the spirit runs to waste; and on the other hand unrelated spiritual example seldom reproduces itself in others." She was feeling for a technique of application.

"I just break up and work hard and am uncomfortable," she told me, "and then I find I am raised up to a super state and in touch with something that I did not have before. I see it vaguely and look back and tell you about it. I don't just sit and read about it and see it; I do it, whatever I'm at. That is why I work so hard and keep quiet so long.

"The way I'm presenting this it sounds so gloomy," she broke off to complain. "But really it is so cheerful, so jolly and so loving and wise and warm-hearted. You see, it isn't any question of going out and trying to be good. There's a great danger in that, because we are apt to lose the exuberance of our sinfulness; and that is taming, very very taming.

What you miss, the way I am telling it, is the EXUBERANCE."

"What's the matter with zest?" suggested the Invisible. "You do not think of muscular 'exercise', for instance, when you experience zest.

You do not iron yourself out into any newly acquired condition. Duty does not drive you to it. Logic is left in storage. With full flow through you proceed to enjoy living. That is spiritual action.

"Of course," they added, "you cannot go around zesting things priggishly. That is not what is meant. What we want to get into these teachings is naturalness, not priggishness." They recurred again and again, in many forms of expression, to the assurance that they demanded of Betty no great and noble tasks. Just living, said they, ordinary daily living. Plenty of material to work on there.

"NOTHING IS TOO SMALL TO WORK ON WITH THE TOOLS OF ETERNAL VALUES," emphasized the Invisibles. "Take the smallest things, little hourly experiences or situations of a commonplace day, you can, by your concentration of desire, transform them into a spiritual significance akin to a poem." The Invisibles' word "poem" set Betty off up a bypath.

"Poetry is thought's most buoyant form, ready for release into emotion," she said to me, with an air of confiding something, I am poetry now. It is the most volatile form of human communication. I am beauty running free, only shaped by the momentary effort to reflect some particularization of life, instead of life itself. Always it is shaping, and the limitations of form are its pain, the ecstasy of its suffering.

"Have you ever thought of the visual body of a poem?" she continued her apparently irrelevant fancies. "How it typifies its buoyancy compared to prose? It floats on a page; it isn't anchored at all the comers.

"I do things so curiously," said Betty after a pause. "I had to do some sordid scrubbing stuff; and then in order to make a poem out of it, I blew some soap bubbles out of the scrubby stuff, and laughed.

"I came over today in a blind and unilluminated state," she continued, back at last to her knitting, "and the first function I felt was of pouring myself out. I think after a while this would get me all the functions I needed... Anyway, if I didn't do it, I wouldn't have much."

## 2.

"I am," on another occasion said Betty with satisfaction, "sort of contained in a general heart-expansion—nice and human—I can't explain it— "I don't think that would make sense," she answered some unspoken suggestion. "The word 'love' doesn't suit my needs; I'll pass it by. I must gather something expressing more vigorous action, less fuzzed up with individuality.

"I'm doing something quite astonishing. There are influences around me radiating the warmth of human affection, only with so much greater power. I dissolve to their love; I surround them as they surround me, steeping in each other's heart-expansion. It's so transforming, breath-taking, and I can't tell you in words. Now, the strange thing is, I reach out and spread this atmosphere around each one I care for. And it enlarges and grows stronger and becomes firm, like a continent in surrounding ocean. Beautiful things are produced on it. I don't understand the rest very well; I'm so puzzled because it's still an individuality. I am that firm body. I feel it in all its part, and yet it is composed of many people. How can that be? I only sense it through the atmosphere of its spaces, as it were." Betty laughed. "That was a funny trick! I went out and brought in a very reluctant one. She had to come!" At the next session the job of giving expression to what seemed to be the inexpressible, was tackled again.

"It's too big to say," Betty confessed at last, "but the only way to get it is the constant struggle to communicate it. I suppose it's hopeless, but I'll try.

"Last time I tried to analyze the different atmosphere I was in, the greater consciousness, which was the substance all of us contain. I was no longer isolated in a small, individual, self-seeking consciousness: I was in an atmosphere of sympathetic attunement with the all. I tried to tell you of that last time. Now I am going on from there.

"The sensation of retaining this atmosphere, of keeping oneself in this higher consciousness, is the means of..." She broke off suddenly.

"I've lost the words," she explained the break. "They were right there, and they got lost. I'll do it over again.

"By means of the heart-expansion people call love, the sensation of super-sympathy—this outflowing and inflowing, this most thrilling and exquisite life—we come the nearest we can to apprehending the conception of God. It can be indulged at any moment of our days, interpenetrating them with universal life. That is the way we intensify our days and harmonize our lives...

"But also there's another element to this atmosphere of heart-expansion which is the universal substance. It's a lifting quality which is the expression of the individual's contact with it. I partake to the greatest possible extent of the heart-expansion. At the same time I sweep on with it, lifting my share of it by means of the energy that is in me. It is as important for me to do my individual part as for the greatest...

"My heart aches with intensity, the atmosphere is so tremendously vital.

You see, this element, which I am admitting by my heart-expansion and which has no words to describe it, is the highest greater-being we are capable of sensing. The more I enter into it, the greater will be my happiness and richness of perception...

"'I know now what that phrase means; God is love. It always sounded so straining and affected to me. I don't like it yet; but that is my stupidity. At least I know what it means. There are so many word—seeds we don't know how to plant and make them grow into life-giving things'"

# 3.

She found it difficult to make an intelligent start in the actual application. Apparently it was to be a repetition, in this field, of her gropings toward realization in others. Again she must arrive at comprehension by cut and try, by the actual doing. But in the doing she found, as always, satisfactions by the way.

"It is a perfumed work," she told me, "like woodsy smells and flowers and odors caught at rare moments. When you lead people out into something they approve of, like Nature, then you can work magic on them." This, I suggested, was poetic but inconclusive.

"Suppose," she countered, "you were set down without equipment in a new world—a world of creative power centered in the individual, what would you do? Today I decided that, to succeed with this power, first of all my fundamental outlook must be one of health, harmony and onward-going success. So I started out trying to experience the difference between times of depression and those of full and overflowing life. I wanted to make myself a strong magic; that is, I wanted to manufacture it for others, for thus only would I call it into being, with reciprocal action on myself.

"Then," said Betty, "I lifted up my desires—after working them into a concrete conception of the desired end according to my limited light. I held them up eagerly and earnestly and continuously, submitting them to the influence above me, and that influence helped me to remodel them to greater perfection and present possession, directed me in the supporting confirmation of what I desired. That's the way to work! "This," said she, with the satisfaction of discovery, "is the application of what I experienced when I with drew inside myself, and shut the door, and staved quiet until I found there was another exit, and so gave my little bit, and the Great Rhythm took it and amplified it. This is the new exit—the rising—above, and all that, is outworn.

"While here," she continued, "I can reach out and quicken the thoughts and hearts of any human being I have ever known. What then? What right have I? How do I dare utilize that power, and for what purpose? I cannot see the answers to these questions now. I only know that one who has experienced this power, even momentarily, can never again be satisfied, as is the walnut in its shell." She lapsed for a time into contemplation of some inner experience. I asked her what she was doing.

"I am going through the sensations of another person regarding this influence," she replied. "He is a person with an absorbing occupation, one that demands all his working hours and energy—just caught in the habit and fixture of days like that. I am that person. That is the wall I am up against. I have to begin with the tiniest little start of some kind and keep working at it..." She was silent for a while.

"Now then! I only had room in my mind for the hopelessness of doing anything else with my days... This isn't me," she reminded, "it's somebody else... Then in a fertile-spirited moment a shred of vision came to me, a tiny fleeting glimpse of a different kind of living.

Suddenly I saw a beautiful radiance, sensed a better scheme; and because it was the real-thing inspiration, because it met the fertile moment in me, it didn't fade out like the worded inspiration in books. It was persistent. A sort of breath of sweet spring growth had come to me in a damp dark dungeon. I was sprouted by it somehow...

"Now what to do? I am back at the beginning. I am seeing that this sprout thing may be only a cellar sprout. It may be only, for a while, at best a potted plant or a window box, instead of a forest giant fighting storms or spreading silent under the starlight...

"At least it's the way EVERYBODY has to begin. Every human being advances by the same path. And the universal experience of it is what satisfies people's minds that, if they are way behind, they must catch up.

"Well, if that is the way to go about it," sighed Betty, somewhat doubtfully, "at least there's something tangible to get at."

# CHAPTER 16

# HABITUAL SPIRITUAL CONSCIOUSNESS

## 1.

It was curious and interesting to me to follow Betty's own change of inner attitude toward the thing she was doing. At the start she worked at it only during the especially dedicated hour or so of formal "communication." Her object was to get "messages." And her chief reaction was of high adventure. But little by little she shifted until her objective became no single concrete thing at a specified time, but a continuous state of mind.

The Invisibles approved strongly of this change in purpose; probably all along they had been working to induce it. The "sessions," with myself attending, were all right, and necessary and must be continued. But they were now only a small part of Betty's job. Hers was the proverbial "woman's work" in that it was never done! She must practice, said the Invisibles, by herself. Not in "psychics," or communicating, or any of the rest of that; but in realizing—making real to herself—this new found inner state. Start first thing in the morning, said they.

"The first business of each day," they told her, "should be a recognition of the sun of your life—unquestioning and eager heart-lifting acknowledgment of the warm, loving, positive creative force of the universe beyond your knowledge. Always give time to purify and clothe fittingly your spirit to contemplate the unknown great Causal Force operating through each living thing. Unless you make a conscious exercise of this, conscious power is not yours throughout the day." And, they emphasized, that power throughout the day must be conscious.

Which, Betty acknowledged, was a fine counsel of perfection, but as a practical matter might be somewhat difficult. Highly desirable to float through the hours on a high plane of serenity, but how about telephone calls, and the cook with her lists, and the arrival of the plumber, and But that was not at all the idea. The Invisibles kept at her, and finally managed to convince her.

"I see," she cried, "each day we must create for ourselves by this magic, call it what you please—tuning, ordering—a dignified temple suitable for the habitation of our highest ideals. It is as though one made of each separate day a beautiful little habitation in which to live while the big temple of the lifetime is building. There is retardment and confusion and discouragement in working out the greater scheme, unless the little temple of each separate day is prepared as an inspirational workroom. You know, workmen on big buildings always have these little houses to work from, but they are generally ugly." Thereafter Betty never omitted these "early morning ablutions," as she called them. Every morning she retired for a half hour to her little sun-room, and nobody was permitted to interfere, not even the cook! Occasionally travel or emergency might prevent. Nevertheless she would always manage to sit quiet, for at least a few minutes, by herself.

## 2.

This procedure was the first step toward establishment of what the Invisibles called "habitual spiritual consciousness." Before long they insisted on another.

"A new field," she reported to me, "almost a business-like field, establishing us in the substance of reality. It has to be done or we'll go no further... Otherwise we would go with the drift of those who just experiment or are content merely to be experimented on." "That sounds like a threat," I commented. "Where might we fall down?" "A subtle dulling of accustomedness," replied the Invisibles. "You must partake more constantly of the vitality within reach. The accumulation of the details of living reduce the power to a minimum." There ensued a short pause.

"The single thing I can get hold of today," Betty said at last, "is the drabness of our life. Why don't we intensify it? It can be so breath-taking and so magically progressive! There are not enough breathing spaces, like parks in a city; not enough moments of susceptibility to happiness and well-being; it's not punctuated; it's all run together with the details of living. If we could only make ourselves distribute more and more frequently through our hours little breathing spaces for the spirit to mount to consciousness of strength and well-being, that would be the training we need in the gradual acquisition of the happiness we won't take. But we shut it out for all but the occasional hour, and gradually the barrier thickens. We must keep it thin and easily broken through. It's the FREQUENCY, not the length of time, that does it. The more frequently, the richer the personality. It is very difficult to fight the tendency to hibernate in the world. Might just as well do it now." "Co-agulation sets in," explained the Invisibles, "if you don't KEEP broken up, if you don't keep listening at the higher pitch. Habituate yourself to it by utilizing it constantly..." "This is confused, very much confused; but that's it", put in Betty.

"Can't find the clear way to put it. It is very bothersome because first a thing seems audible and then visible; but in reality it is all the same sense over here, and you can't tell which is which when you are separating them into word-senses. It's a reality of FEEL. This is like having too many legs: it's a nuisance— a two legged animal explaining loco-motion to a centipede. It is very confusing to have so many senses...

"But anyway," resumed the Invisibles, "all you've got to remember is that when you make an effort you generate a spark which helps you to enter intermittently that higher more intensive form of life where sparks live. The oftener you do it, the more you get. When you decide it isn't worth while, and is too much trouble, you get out of hearing distance..." "Hold on! " I objected. "You are talking sparks now. How can you hear sparks?" "Out of reach, then," amended the Invisibles, you get where you think sparks are just impractical, imaginative and impossible. And so you cheat yourself." A few sessions later they brought the whole proposition more into the clear.

"The time has come," said they, "when the thing we have been calling spiritual contact must penetrate into the more practical. It must be elongated, as it were, to touch more commonplace conditions of mind.

The effort is now to gain a more particularized method of maintaining the growth already made, to gain the constant refreshment necessary to keep the spiritual life vigorous.

"Make three and four minute sessions during the whole day whenever you have an interval. Make it the most vital necessity of your day. At present you are giving us leftover time, and that is discouraging and retrogressive. The every-day-every-hour attitude of mind is so much more useful than any amount of periodical concentration! "The main thing," continued the Invisibles, "is to keep sweeping back and forth, so the dividing line between the two worlds doesn't show.

Commute all the time: it's easy if you keep in practice. It's a definite proposition—as definite as keeping outside your shell. That shell is a very exact symbol. Once allow your consciousness to slip into it, and you are at home and familiar and comfortable, recognizing nothing tangible but its commonplaces. Keep out of it! Train yourself to be at home outside—to occupy, ordinarily, daily, hourly, the highest consciousness you have achieved.

"A little reiteration will not hurt. It's the carrying through idea: HABITUAL CONSCIOUSNESS.'"

# 3.

Betty did not acquire readily the ease of spirit she ultimately gained.

In spite of her new understanding she sometimes found it difficult to cope with the common distractions—travel, illness, house-guests, sheer inertia—and most of all the trivial, accustomed routine of daily living.

Little things, often repeated, gain a momentum that is hard to break or check. But slowly her compass swung toward the desired orientation.

"It is a very interesting experience I am going through," she commented, "pruning and rearranging, selecting, stimulating life's directions. So much falling from me, so much expanding before me. My eager impulse towards the things dimly sensed and greatly desired outruns my laboriously slow accomplishment. My heavy self doesn't cooperate with my active spiritual being." By this time Betty was pretty well at home in her disassociated state.

The first struggle for re-establishment was over, but the struggle in the tangible world was just beginning.

"When I'm here, I enjoy myself," she announced one day from that other consciousness. "But I am exalted above the confirmation of my powers.

And I don't know how to confirm them so they will be enduring. It's as if someone had clothed me in most distinguished estate, and I go in it rather ignobly conscious that it does not belong to me—that I am not fit for it. And I am ashamed not to deserve the beauty and dignity, instead of merely presenting the externals of it." "What's the trouble? " I asked. "Aren't you getting along fast enough to suit you?" "I still get only glimpses of the great power I talk about and which I am struggling to comprehend," she explained. "Of course, I enter the higher level with increasing frequency. There is no question about it: normal consciousness is assuming lesser proportions. But there is pain in the contrasts I suffer. It is so confusing to overlap the two consciousnesses! just now, for instance, I was establishing myself comfortably—so happy and busy and settled about myself. And then the other focus of my consciousness showed up and said it was intangible stuff. But it is not. Dear me! It is most annoying to have two focuses. What am I to do?" She worked on her problem.

"It is as if I were building something and had just established the corner of the top layer," she continued presently. "And then I stopped there and went away, and lived in an entirely different level! I've simply got to make that my home, just as the lower level is now. I've got to live in it and finish it out. There is no use starting it unless you live in it. That just postpones your destiny. That is the trouble with all of us: we keep our ideals as lookout towers, and we seldom take the trouble to climb the stairs." For a long interval Betty was silent. Then, in a puzzled tone: "Something is growing in me and has put out a shoot. Maybe this physical world is only our roots. Maybe a Plant is terribly worried over its first shoot." Another long pause.

"Now," she asserted suddenly, "instead of REACHING up, I have MOVED up.

I am staying there. It works, too! Again the pause.

"Ah, that's grand! " she cried at last, in triumph. "That's a real vista! I WILL NOT HAVE the horrid little near-sighted, cramped, strained half-breathed atmosphere of the lesser life. I won't have it! I am going to do my work with a well-ventilated mind, continually conscious of the lifting power of deep-breathed perceptions. I am not going to IN-HABIT my lower level. I am the better workman if I center myself in other regions." She broke off, and for some moments was still.

"I'm coming back," she ended. "Do you know, my body seems like a troublesome child to me now. I drag it around, and bathe it, and dress it, and stand it, and sit it, and fuss over it!"

# 4.

"It is most important," pointed out the Invisibles to Betty, "that you do not get a misconception of what we intend to convey by the term 'habitual spiritual consciousness.' This does not imply any retirement into any permanent state of abstraction, nor any priggish watchfulness to determine that your every move is transcendental. It means simply that each day, when you finish your practice, you do not close the experience like a book, but carry it around like a treasured possession.

Instead of being completely forgotten, it remains in the back of your mind, communicating its influence automatically to your actions and reactions, and ready at any moment, if specifically called upon, to lend a helping hand.

"It is particularly necessary, perhaps, to distinguish this state clearly from the periods of intense concentration you employ for training and development. In especial exercises such as these, you are for a purpose temporarily focusing on certain aspects of yourself.

During these periods you impose on the other aspects your command that they sit still and do not bother you, so to speak, until you have finished. You totally—or as nearly so as possible—inhibit their activities. You dismiss all reports from the subconscious; you clear the conscious mind of thought.

"But when you invoke the higher consciousness in the course of normal daily living you do not do this. The bodily functions proceed with no less, and no more, than your customary awareness of them. Your brain-mind moves forward on its unintermitting stream of thoughts and mental images. A bodily or mental vacuum is unnatural and impossible. To check the flow of these things is also unnatural, and allowable only for a special purpose. Whole living implies the simultaneous functioning of all the parts of yourself. Only the sharp focus of your attention is shifted as desired to that portion of your being where it is important that it should function for the business of the moment.

"You must at all times remember, however, that it is as serious a mistake to concentrate wholly in the superconscious as it is in the brain-mind or the body. To each its balanced due of yourself; for that balancing is the art of life."

# CHAPTER 17

# THE HIGHER POWER

"I go to the Source," said Betty, summing up her own practise. "In doing so I utilize my higher mind, abandon myself to my intuitional, secure in its reality. I give up looking at the Source externally. I try to enter into its feeling of power and strength. After I do this a little while, I am no longer an alien thing. I am somehow attached to it sympathetically. Then I keep quiet, very happily and expectantly, and its potentiality seeks in me some little entrance, some crack or cranny through which I receive some little bit. But that little bit does its work. Eventually that bit must be recognized in my own medium for some definite purpose. Now I am magnetized with it; one with it. But finally I have to come out on the borderline, and I take back with me only just as much as will fit into the customary mind's capacity for statement.

"Sometimes," she confessed, "I get sort of thwarted and bored. I have to get over that." She sought for the way to increase her capacity.

"I am trying to look at the Source and understand it for you," said she.

"It's a kind of disembodied quality. I am on the power side, and being assisted temporarily by great strength and wisdom. Under its spell I'm turning to look down to see why I don't get more of it ordinarily.

"All of us—our group—have had a hazy conception that there are such things as spiritual forces that work just as well as our physical forces do, only superlatively. We all admit them, but still our hands and eyes and legs and ears are of far more utility to us. The disembodied quality I am now looking at is what would give us actual possession of the working ability of these higher forces. This quality is not much recognized. Actually it is just the SURENESS OF YOUR BELIEF IN THE EXISTENCE OF THIS GREATER FORCE. That is the principal thing to begin with.

"Take an example from natural physical forces. You wouldn't have the nerve or the idiocy to try walking on water; but you step out on ice with perfect confidence. In ordinary daily living you come to associate your mind so naturally and pleasurably and habitually with the forces which control our physical universe that they grow measurably firm under the feet, as it were. Take gravitation, which always works; the magnetic attraction or the power of electricity when control is established; the buoyancy of placement in water—any of the natural laws that appeal to you. Our conscious minds approve and abandon all test of them.

"But these higher forces we have sensed only as weak generalizations.

We've got to make them the same in our conscious minds as the natural forces I mentioned, and which we accept as a matter of course. We've got to associate with them, experiment with them, as constantly and interestedly as people did in uncovering the laws controlling the physical forces. The same practice will make our spiritual bodies work.

Anyway, it's the first necessity we shall be faced with when we 'go hence.' Everything we have been accustomed to will have gone away from us. If we haven't built this extension of confidence in the new forces, we shall be at a loss. This particular attitude of mind, surety, confidence is ITSELF a force: it IS a superlative force." "What we are stepping around," said the Invisibles, "is to avoid the use of the word 'faith.' We don't want to use it until we have freshened it.

It's been made respectable by calling it suggestion: you all know the power of that. Only this is its pure reality, its ESSENCE." There was a short pause.

"They told me I couldn't get much of it," Betty resumed, "only enough to begin with. I'll tell you how I'm doing it.

"I made a sort of cradle of confidence of the tides and the moon and the planetary swings; and I said, there's no reason why I shouldn't rest this spirit of me securely in these unfailing forces. I felt delightfully in suspension, restful with everlasting—arms restfulness.

This extension of my personality, the reality I call myself, has quite reasonably ventured out to associate with unseen but thoroughly tested realities. That's the beginning that is how we begin to grow into the higher forces.

"I have a funny way of working. I vary all kinds of tests. I jump up and down on these bigger laws to feel their reality. Mentally I turn and twist them all, and jiggle them around, and they still hold me up with a sureness of cause and effect.

"Now I will leave that testing side for a minute and just seek the SOCIETY of the greater forces." A long silence followed.

"Feels sort of like a blind person walking along," said Betty at last.

"I know by the feeling when I get in a sunspot of power, and I try to keep in it, and when I stray out of it I try to get back. I know it's there, and I just have to make my senses so acute that I can keep in it or get back to it if I stray.

"Each person must play his own mental game in this thing. I am only suggesting mine...

"All this is an effort to establish us firmly in the spiritual so we can utilize its greater powers in doing the physical things we see are worth doing. This definite belief in a force assisting our best efforts, and our reckoning on its unfailing help; the establishment of this principle of the constructive, directive forward movement which we call evolution—this condition of faith must at some time or other in our progression be permanently accepted by our united being." "Now the point is this," stated the Invisibles, "there exists in you, indefinitely developable, an engine of power, dynamically creative, capable of impressing and moulding your material world according as you give out from your inner being its creative force. This force is not primarily the MENTALLY creative force, which you understand perfectly.

It is, as it were, a higher sense of that mentally creative force; in short the vital principle of life. It comes, not from that mere agent of the soul, the intellect, but from the plexus of life itself. Mental force can make a mould or plan, but for completion this plan must have the vital principle supplied. Mental force is the neatly made electric globe into which the current is not turned. The true creative force, on the other hand, carries its own vital principle with it. It is a matter of the heart as well as the clearly seen concept of the mind." Betty groped for definition in words—and as always she was dissatisfied.

"I'm trying," Betty said, "to get a clear idea of this spreading, creative, radiant thing I'm associating with. It is a supporting force pertaining to the reach just above us. I like to get in it and be swept along with it, but I don't think I'm ready. It goes on to such a vast ocean beyond my comprehension...

"It's so nameless I don't know where to begin to cut it up into words.

If I do that, I'm afraid it won't piece together again. It's too big for language. All I can say is that it's the biggest union of life, the nearest to harmony, the most collected force...

"Harmony is so poor a word! It isn't a BAD word; it's just a mistreated word. I want to give FRESHNESS to that word. Now it's just a semi-religious, semi-musical term; but really there is a rising tide of progress connected with it. Well, in spite of its inadequacy it represents a strong factor in this force that upholds, this tide of extension. But it is not the thing itself—only a shred.

"The thing itself is not will-power, either; that's only another aspect of it; just one more place where we've touched it in comprehension. What I am trying to get at is the whole of this force; not only the detached bits we recognize in words of will-power and concentration, but the complete power of it." "There is always a contracted and an expanded form of everything," contributed the Invisibles. "Willpower is the contracted form of this higher thing. You can step into it from will-power without contracting if on think of it more as DESIRE-POWER. Will-power is in spite of your desires." One day Betty—more or less in desperation, I suspect—tried the label of "pure feeling". But she recoiled from it at once. The phrase had been too much knocked about by sentimentality.

"Some day," said she, "I'm going to take pure feeling and cleanse it of the taint of transient emotion, weak sentiment, because pure feeling is the divine spark. It is the intelligence of the heart, the secret of creative magic. Pure feeling is a warrior quality. It is made of the stuff that endures. Strong and true, it engages with earth passions and comes through them unscathed. Still I despair of setting down pure feeling." But the Invisibles found the phrase acceptable enough, for the time being, at least.

"Pure feeling, " said they "cannot be apprehended by the brain. You can, however, cultivate it by welcoming its entrance into your heart region.

Experiment, and see how it softens all the cruel rigidities of life, how it escapes all chains and shackles of maladjustments." Betty paused long to consider, and perhaps to experiment.

"I made the most superhuman effort to muse myself to the possibilities I have been shown," she reported at last. "And I struggled and struggled with increasing difficulty until I remembered the secret of the heart-solvent. Then a great, warm rushing sensation came over me, and in the stimulation of it I longed unspeakably to be able to make the effort and do the work, to assume the responsibilities pertaining to the distinguished estate that has been loaned me. In this great rush of vitality resulting from just the right combination of life I actually sensed creative BLOOD coursing through me. And that gave me the feeling of the only way to work toward permanent occupancy." "Why not," suggested the Invisibles, "think of the higher force as a compound of the ESSENCES of all the qualities of all the forms of life and experience one encounters? And then, in imagination, select and call forth those particular essences one needs for the use of any particular moment in life? "That's a good game," said they. And Betty, with her usual enthusiasm for games, pounced upon it at once.

"If I am to work in essences," said she, "I must get the tools of my craft. So I collect myself essences: the energy of my waterfalls, the stability of my rock, the time achievement of my trees—there is such inspiration in their achievement in time. I like their beauty of age.

When I stand under a big tree, I am glad I am growing old! I want that kind of garnered strength. I want trees and waterfalls and big rocks.

They are so real in themselves. The realities of humans tire me—their wars, murders, shortsightedness.

"Thus I collect essences. All I have to do is to walk in my garden collecting and releasing essences—never hoarding in the cloistered-garden sense. Essences are everywhere to work with.

"It would take a poet or an angel to express it," she said at last, "because we do not know how to partake of this super-happiness. I get just a breath of it when I lie down next the earth and sniff it; and I get just a taste of it when I come in on the waves and the salt is on my lips; and I get just a whisper of it when I stay still in the woods and listen; and I get the most of it when I love something, even my dog or my garden. Don't you see; I want so much to sink deep, dive, be absorbed in this intense reciprocity, this thing I can't even name. It must be experienced and entered completely in order to have practical understanding and sympathy and accomplishment in the material world. It gives an endless vista..."

# CHAPTER 18

# THE SOURCE OF SUPPLY

We have now, you and I together in these pages, travelled many miles along the Road that Betty knew. Through her eyes of the spirit we have seen much of the landscape it traverses; and in her company we have passed certain landmarks, and have risen to certain heights from which we can see the highway going on for eternity, as the Invisibles had once said. And somehow, though we cannot discern the end of the Road, we are able to make out, through the mists, at least the lay of the land through which Betty will continue her journey.

What lies about us at this point? Aside from all the details of instruction and the by-products of acquisition, I think I should define as the kernel of her accomplishment up to now, conscious contact, or tuning in at will, With the Source.

What of this Source? In extreme starkness of definition, it is the vital principle that is the basis of all manifestations and energies that make up the universe.

It is the underlying evolutionary power, force, life that makes things, and keeps them in being, in development, and in functioning. The highest expression of this force on earth indubitably is human consciousness.

And so an extended definition leads up to Consciousness as the one and only reality. We sense this highest of reality, but not broken into bits as is our own experience, but all-inclusive—and all knowing.

Some people name it God: some people name it something else. That does not matter.

Now if Betty had stopped, on her road, at the milestone of mere contact, she would have found herself in a numerous company. Mystic communion has been often enough achieved to be generally recognized, even if not widely practiced. But such mere contact does not get you to the end of the journey. Betty's next forward thrust was to be toward another milestone, not so well known.

The Source is the vital principle of which we must partake for mere being. It is the origin, cause, basis of existence. But merely to exist is not enough. Creation must also function. To function it must have energy, power. And that energy and power, certainly so far as we are concerned, must be renewed as it exhausts itself by use. That is an axiom we well know as applying to, say, a gasoline engine. It has a fuel tank, which must from time to time be refilled.

But now we are called upon to discover that renewal is a universal need.

The vast machine that is creation in cosmos, that is the earth and all that in it is, that is OURSELVES, must have its power, and it must be renewed. Otherwise all sits "numb, and dumb and unaware," awaiting the Word.

Ask any man what he seeks from life. Happiness, he will reply. And of what substance is happiness? Why, his first thought runs, bodily health and comfort and efficiency, and a certain security of possessions. But soon, even though he gains them in full measure, he must conclude that these things are not happiness. His discontents are not for things outside. His hunger is for things within.

What does man really want, in the unstable world of today? Mental peace, I think. But mental peace seems to him out of reach in high inexpressibles, on which he cannot put his finger. And yet, if he could analyze, they are not so many. A few things would suffice—to achieve his ambitions, and perhaps a little more; to gain an inner assurance of a stability that is independent of outward circumstance; above all to possess both the faith and the FEELING that there is a strength beyond his own, and that he can command and utilize it.

There is that strength, Betty was assured. We do tap it and utilize it.

But ordinarily our tapping it is unconscious, a mere prerequisite of any function at all. We take from it only what the need of the moment forces upon us, so to speak, and in consequence our existence is niggardly and hampered.

So there is the Source, not only of being, but of power—the Source of Supply.

Nobody would lead a niggardly and hampered existence if he could help it. Well, he can help it, Betty demonstrates. It is unnecessary. No man need be content with only just enough to get by with. If he would follow her Road he will discover that it is possible for him to tap the Source of Supply as a conscious and intended act. And in so doing he will find that what he can take from that Source of Supply is limited only by his desire-power and the energy with which he is willing to back it! For the Source of Supply is unfailing and inexhaustible. And sympathetic and understanding.

What is the practical value of this knowledge? Where does one apply it in everyday living? Merely to acquire it is not sufficient: one must accomplish. How? The answer is engraved on Betty's next milestone.

At the point in her progress to which we have now traced her Betty had entered fully into the occupation and savor of her "private world" and its powers and prerogatives. She had perfected her mystic communion with the Source. She had learned how to tap the Source of Supply. But now she perceived that she was to be not the owner, but the agent. She must learn how to be the agent. That was the next stretch of her Road she must traverse.

From the Source of Supply, Betty was told, we can get everything, unstinted, EVERYTHING that is good for us and that we have earned and deserve. BUT ONLY PROVIDED WE KNOW HOW to GIVE IT AWAY AFTER WE GET IT! "Take no thought of the morrow—" "All things shall be added unto you—" But why? And how? Betty's contribution from here on was to be not so much the discovery of additional principles, as the learning of how to manage the fundamentals she had already mastered. Let us follow her progress on this next stretch of her Road.

# CHAPTER 19

# THE GREAT SIMPLICITIES

## 1.

By nature Betty was a giving person. Indeed, I used to joke that her endless generosities had forced me to become mean and avaricious just to keep us out of the poorhouse. There was little need, therefore, for the Invisibles to stress DESIRE as the first rule in the discipline of outflow. Nonetheless outflow, as well as inflow, must be motivated, they told us, by the wish—to rather that the will—to. And Betty, the naturally generous and free handed, responded with enthusiasm. "It's so much more natural to give," she said, "than to take." Not that there were no gropings and stumblings on the way to her full understanding of the art of managing the outflow of the Supply, now that she had learned how to tap it. There were many puzzlements. But these the Invisibles helped her to resolve by what they called the Great Simplicities.

I shall not catalogue the Simplicities here in advance, but rather call them to attention as they developed in due course. It is best to picture Betty as reaching out for them, feeling her path as she went—for that is how it actually happened.

"There come certain times in one's evolution when one completes a phase of development," Betty was explaining the next stretch of road.

"Instead of being a freshman, one is a senior. I can always tell when I am starting a new field of work, because I can turn around so easily and look back at the old one so clearly. And you can't turn around until you have pretty well finished up a stage...

"I wish I could get a good analogy for the sensation of what I'm facing now. There's quite a change in the FEEL of it—something like being made a pro instead of an amateur." Contributed the Invisibles: "The PRACTICE of the higher consciousness, an ACTIVE life regulated by it—this is the final step in our present teachings. After accustoming yourself to the universal mind, convincing yourself of its desirability, then comes the still more difficult practice of using it. It must be done in relation to earth life, or it is not done at all. One must learn to take the rough and tumble, the unsympathetic contacts, indifferent if not actually thwarting." There was a pause while Betty digested this.

"Formerly," she acknowledged at last, "I brought myself, by various symbols to stand under a spiritual sun, as it were, passive and receptive. Now I must go out actually on the earth to live to the full, to fail and fall, experiment, create a new environment..." "You admit the inflow unquestioningly," said the Invisibles. "That, however, is but an opening of the gates. You must go THROUGH." "Oh dear, I've been so busy getting this thing into my consciousness," lamented Betty, "and now I've got to be just as busy getting it out—and it's just as hard!" "Remember," reiterated the Invisibles, "the first point—that the active life means constant inflowing and outflowing. You must never, never forget to be constantly giving out.

Either Betty or myself—I forget which—wanted a specific hint as to where to begin. Active where and how? "It doesn't make the least difference what you do," came the answer, "or which part of the world you choose to function in. It is the functioning itself that counts. The main thing is to get rid of the stoppage at the place of meeting with the world. The 'through' process MUST be acquired.

"Without this giving out there is no circulation. From now on YOUR OUTGO MUST EQUAL YOUR INTAKE. You"—they were speaking more directly to Betty—"are rapidly outgrowing the stage where you contain, as a quiet pool, a backwater portion of the current of life. In future your status must be one of continuous movement, without stoppage at your point of contact with the world. Obstruction is there at present.

"Don't be so solemn about it," they urged. "This is a pleasure-giving party, solely and simply an acceleration of happiness—and how to step on the accelerator. That doesn't make such a bad picture, does it?"

And anyway, they pressed the point home, how do you get fun out of anything you have? "By using it," they insisted. "You can have titles of possession, but they are only scraps of paper. Can't you imagine a man who doesn't know how to read, owning a library with every book in the world in it? All he owned would be STUFF. He couldn't eat it. He couldn't get ANYTHING out of it! "The important thing to realize is that this unified consciousness cannot be imprisoned and shackled. It must be held lightly and loaned to others, passed freely and lavishly. One's function is to HELP CONDUCT A FLOW—not to steal a cupful of something and ran away with it. I thought the Invisibles were rather over-stressing the point. Still they tried for a clearer picture, as Betty slowly took their dictation, seemingly hanging on every word.

"It is a sort of down-thrust after the upward extension," said they, "a definite MOVEMENT in return. Whatever you practice hereafter, keep in mind the strong down-thrust as necessary for rebound.

"In fact, there is little permanent value in having learned the higher laws unless you can do this. Suppose with their help you have succeeded in transmuting an area around yourself—have made a start at surrounding yourself with harmony and health and happiness. Still you haven't really accomplished much unless you can maintain the effectiveness of your perception by spreading the area. That area, that transmutation, must spread, expand around you, or you will find yourself possessed only of narrow puritanical piety." So it was then that Betty mastered one of the Great Simplicities—Circulation, as the Invisibles now and then called it, meaning not merely the necessity for an outgo equal to the intake. The outgiving must not be intermittent. Circulation, not in spurts but rather as a continuous flow-movement always; that's the idea.

"I see myself as I used to be," said Betty finally, "convinced of the essential tuning process, without which we are nothing; doing it more or less regularly; luxuriating in it even. The picture is now repellent to me. It lacked something I must temporarily name robustness and independence. It had no joyous dynamics. It would be impossible for me to return to the apathetic stage, except periodically for rest, or if I became conscious of nervous tensions, or for healing if ill. No longer am I concerned with exercises in spiritual contact. That, fortunately, has become automatic. I've made that connection. Now I've got to turn the current on and let it flow through. Circulation!"

# 2.

Particularization was the name given by the Invisibles to another of the Great Simplicities.

"A rather ponderous bit of language," I suggested.

Betty chuckled, as though she too had found the word amusing. But her amusement quickly passed. There was a long pause.

"I must try to tell you," she said at last, "what I experienced just now in being unable to utilize the love force around me. I could not hold it condensed and shape it in any form. I must explain this, because we've got to understand it—the pain of taking shape, the anguish of particularization. I have no right to take more expansion. It would be like overfeeding, or massed wealth—something damaging to me. I have been allowed for years to experience the rhapsody of a higher life, but now I come willingly to suffer the pain of myself shaping one little verse from the great rhapsody...

"Don't you see, I've progressed to beauty and abundance but can't enjoy it because there's no scheme or plan of arrangement to it." She fell silent a moment.

"Take a concrete example from our everyday lives," she continued. "Let us say we have decided that our days are going to be shaped in freedom of movement, unbarnacled. And suppose we have acquired the expansion of heart, and are trying to live it widely and glowingly and merrily. Now we come to the point: there is something more than that. If we stop there, it is almost a stagnation. We have got to be continually taking those very qualities of liberation and wide sympathy, and shaping them into something needed in the world, something near to others. This we must do, even at the cost of suffering diminutions of our emotional satisfaction." Mere outflow, it seemed, was not enough, however sustained and steady.

It must focus to definite ends; it must particularize.

"Inspiration," said the Invisibles, "comes only in attraction to some definite output, some definite production. It CANNOT come unless it has a container. Inspiration only fills what is prepared for it. It cannot be controlled otherwise. It is like electricity; it has to be brought into a mechanism ready for it. The through current must push something.

In the same way the higher consciousness is a wonderful driving force, but its nature is to dissipate unless it meets something that helps its particularization. The force WANTS to be assisted: it comes for that purpose. Remember that: it is a waiting, undifferentiated force THAT

WANTS TO BE DIFFERENTIATED. Your business is now to attach something to it—and so make it practical.

"At first your little stream will doubtless find its way only in diffused efforts hither and thither, seeking a path in which to flow.

But just as Water tends to unify itself in a river bed, so you too must feel your way to a shaping." "I don't shoot straight ahead with a superior overriding force," interjected Betty. "I hardly even plan. I seem at first just to stand tiptoe and look ahead at my objective, at it were. Then I busy myself generating a great and composed secure determination, quite different from nervous will-power. It is a great confident recognition of my ability to get there. Only I seem to work very hard at the generating; as if I actually made light, where it was dark, in order to see the way.

Oh, I can't seem to say anything that fits." And then she added, chuckling again: "I feel like a smudge pot, keeping off the frost. That's all I can do now... Well, it's something! It helps the climate—temporarily."

# 3.

In the enthusiasm of this outflowing, warned the Invisibles, Betty was not to forget to keep up the inflow. That is the trouble with so many people.

"As water evaporates under the influence of the sun," said the Invisibles, "so does the absorbing quality of earth life diminish your supply. Keep ever in mind the constant uninterrupted renewal of power.

Have complete confidence in the power house, of which you are a distributor.

"Evaporation of force is so subtly accomplished that you may not always recognize your depletion," they, continued. "So keep constantly in mind the power house idea, making sure you possess its feeling of strength before attempting to distribute—or combat. There is grave danger here of ill equipment and defeat for no reason but the world-sapping of your strength, of which you have been unconscious. If your weapons fail you, it is because you have allowed this. Distribution is so easy and comfortable when you feel sure of the storage capacity." But don't worry about it, the Invisibles added. It is not going to desert you, in the interims, provided you do return regularly to the power house.

"Don't keep wondering if you are 'working in a spiritual way,' " they said. "The Source will not desert you unless you lose your surety and strangle yourself with tensions. Then you cut it off; you chill yourself. The important thing is the sensing how long you can work masterfully without renewing yourself." "It cannot be just abandoned," Betty joined in. "Yet we do not keep nervously busy maintaining it." "It is Your rhythm that is important," the Invisibles returned. "There is nothing difficult about it. Just do not go on working when you feel that depreciation has set in. Then a momentary return to attunement is all that is necessary; PROVIDED you have made a strong and accustomed home of it, have established your home of comfort and worship." And that momentary return to attunement constituted still another of the Great Simplicities—REPLENISHMENT.

"Like using a storage battery which has to be recharged," was my suggestion. "Isn't it possible to connect up with the dynamo?" "Yes," they again agreed, "—ultimately. But right now we are trying to set down a kindergarten way. And the two outstanding points of it are: to spend always plenty of time tuning yourself in comfort and worship at your Source, plenty of time to well establish your participation in its power, replenishing it when need be; and then never to doubt that it follows you when your MIND is completely freed from it in the minutiae of work." "It's a handhold for practice in turmoils, even little turmoils," confided Betty. "I am trying to get something clear-cut for the rough and tumble of things. You are apt to send out then a sort of desperate feeler for something you think you have lost. You feel that you ought to be doing something different and extra-special about something you left behind you. I want to do away with that. If you are running a car at high speed, you can't afford to look up rapturously for inspiration.

You've got to trust the stars are still there, and that you can look up to them when the night comes. You must keep your compartments organized, so you can step from one to the other with no fuzzy places between." "It is," said Betty to me, when finally she had grasped the distinction, "simple technique. The very first thing always is the tuning of yourself, your leap or levitation of heart to your Source;—or even just presenting yourself. It is especially the feeling of comfort. It is, first, the absolute tuning of yourself. You are then imbedded in something so much more potent than yourself, so incomprehensibly secure.

All you can do is to sense the comfort, the security of it; to lend yourself rapturously to it; to worship it.

"Next, while you are completely comfortable, composed and warmed and reassured of your divinity;—while you are there, before any tensions can start, while power is upon you, decide what you are going to do when you are farther away from it; when you have changed your focus. Decide what you are going to do; and go promptly and do it." Not that following the prescription is easy. It was not so even for Betty.

"At present I am working under the greatest difficulty I have ever had," she said. "You see, I used to be like a reservoir with no sluice gates.

Consequently I just overflowed automatically, without control, and a lot went to waste. No longer helped to a super-abundance, I now have to make my own current by opening definite outlets. As a result, what used to be a great outpouring is now only a thin trickle." "Be content," advised the Invisibles. "Keep replenishing. Keep going. It is yours, however pitiful. Beginnings are always pitiful. But that is your stage in the great progression. There is nothing unusual about it.

You are bringing in a substance that is alien to the environment. Be faithful to it. If for long periods it does not augment, what matter? It is there; and in time, with the growth of wisdom, you will find skill for a full flow."

# 4.

"I take stock of myself," Betty told me. "My, but it's nice to be free! If I could only feel this way all the time Nobody ever told me what a tremendous passionate joy there is in pouring yourself out; a necessity of being. I've pent myself up all my life in comparison with what I might have done. It is everything I ever hoped for, life and love and food and drink, outpoured in a great heart-emptying, rush."— And then, another time, years later: "Supposing you offered yourself completely and eagerly, joyously spent yourself on something because you wanted to more than anything else in the whole wide world; and while doing it you suddenly found you were receiving something beyond anything you had ever experienced before, so that you didn't know whether you were giving or taking; that would be the beautiful state, the beautiful union, this wonderful thing we are trying to get hold of and are evolving toward."

# 5.

A very disturbing time had descended on Betty.

"Oh dear! " she cried. "What I don't know worries me so much, and what I do know doesn't interest me! Always, always this feeling of the vastness of what we have to learn. Why sometimes I can glimpse down centuries ahead; and I come back feeling as though I were now in the cave-man age! "That's neither here nor there," she checked herself sharply. "There's no excuse for being fuzzy!" Promptly the fourth Great Simplicity came through. Apparently "spirituality" can and sometimes does get out of hand. It needs REGULATION. So the fourth Simplicity was named.

"The proportioning mechanism is sincerity," decided Betty, after due consideration. "The strength of one's sincerity is a large ingredient of success. That seems to regulate the flow back and forth from the Source to our desired accomplishment. Sincerity. That is the best I can do for that beautiful ingredient of reality. If I said earnestness, it would be dreary and laborious I don't want to get the idea of fixity of any kind, but I WANT TO GET THE IDEA OF REGULATION FROM WITHIN ONE'S SELF. You see, part of the time we shall be using this intuitive leap to the Source and back; and part of the time we shall be using the logic and observation and experience of our ordinary minds. The two come closest together in sincerity. There you are true to both sides, neither lending yourself too loosely to your newly, found visions, nor bringing in the stiffness of your limited mind. So the best I can do is the word sincerity." "Nobody," said the Invisibles, "has ever tarnished it because so few use it completely. It is being yourself, your best inner self, so naturally and freely that you give courage to the timid inner selves of others.

That makes the hook-up. That is offering something simple and sound and true, instead of irritating people with benign shallowness." "It carries so illuminatingly, like a beam across the whole surface of social insincerity." Betty took it up. "It is not bluntness: it is kindly penetration.

"There is also humor, thank goodness!" she added. "That comes in when we limp a little, or lag. It patches up bad holes in our character. It keeps our admirations fresh, because it cannot associate with priggishness. There is always the cheering absurdity between our aims and our nebulous accomplishments. It minimizes our afflictions. It keeps us tender toward the weaknesses of others.

"With Sincerity and Humor we cannot go far wrong, even in untried fields. That's why I call them regulators, these qualities."

# 6.

All this preparation, as presented here, appears to precede the actual experiences and experiments that enabled Betty to realize, to make-it-so, to BECOME what she KNEW. But from the bald chronological standpoint these actual experiences had already long since begun.

However, bald chronology, as always, gives no clear picture of process.

I must, like the Invisibles, skip about, selecting from the record, sketch what seems necessary to the framework of effort and indicate the tools Betty must use. One of the latter, of course, was the care of the physical body. As a furtherance for spiritual development the Invisibles had no use whatever for the medieval idea, still persistent enough, of the "mortification of the flesh." "One thing to respect always," they protested any such point of view, "is the physical body. If there is flattening out and dulling of it, that comes about through various misinterpretations of the relations between the spiritual and the physical. The growth in refinement of the inner being may interpret itself into aenemia of the physical being, into restrictions of foods and appetites of all kinds. Don't make hard and fast rules for yourself physically. Deliberately break over your regulations and observe the reflex of comfort and fluidity your whole being will enjoy. There is no necessity to elaborate this. It is a hint that you can accept or reject as you please." The idea met no opposition from Betty. Zest of enjoyment in all that the world had to offer had always been characteristic of her.

"I want common ordinary earth brute force!" she declared. "It's my contribution, my share. Spirituality on earth is impotent without it. It is the functioning body of the spirit. They concentrate me on the spiritual until I have a certain amount, and then I have to produce the force to make it function. If I merely kept on with the spiritual I'd just get a weak thing that would convince nobody. Oh, I like looking at such nice, fine, forceful bodies! Their muscles stand out; they're fit and ready; and each holds up steadily and blithely his spiritual gift that he is carrying. Fine! It thrills me." Fine! the Invisibles echoed. But, they rather humorously anti-climaxed Betty's abandon, mere physical brute force is not quite it. There is no reason why one should not "be his age," no reason to pretend a physical vigor unnatural to one's years. Let the kids have their own kind of vigor. It's about all they do have! "Attainment of the higher consciousness," the Invisibles pointed out, "involves a new way of working. It has more dependence on mental and spiritual vigor than on physical. The former is not possible in physical youth. You enter a rare period of enjoyment once you can overleap the largely magnified dictates of the body and learn wisely to manage it; learn not to arouse its combative simulations, but to give it ease and consideration, exceptionally pampering it if necessary to gain its cooperation. Let your vigor and abandon of youth, your enthusiasm for adventure, be in the mental and spiritual integration you have acquired.

The body, thus cajoled, will serve you efficiently to the end. Even invalids have acquired this technique for exceptional adventures." Simplicity of all simplicities—respect for the Temple of the Body!

# CHAPTER 20

# THE NATURE OF THE SUBSTANCE

## 1.

The Invisibles never appeared concerned about any difficulties Betty was having. It always seemed to me that they watched her experiments and struggles much as a benign adult watches a baby trying to find out how to fit a peg into a hole. They supplied the peg and the board with the hole in it, and occasionally they dropped a hint on how to get them together, but that was all.

Betty was at a phase of development which the Invisibles ironically called "the tinhorn-rattle-whistle stage of children playing games." But they hastened to add: "The games of children are among their best means of learning. Grown-ups do not play with toys; but taking away a child's toy does not make him a grown-up." Apparently this idea gave Betty pause for thought.

"Over here," she had to agree, rather ruefully, "I am always saying. 'Let's see if I can do it! Let ME do it!' as a child says." "All right, here comes opposition," said the Invisibles. "Get ready! What to do?" "I must gird myself joyously, like a game." Betty rose to the suggestion. "Well, it's my turn! A hard ball is coming! On your toes!" "Using the higher force," said they, "actually is like trying to putt a golf ball down, or to hit a bull's-eye. You have a certain power, and you try to work it; and you figure why you failed, and you try again—just like your sports over there." Of a cold fact it was like our sports over here, Betty told me, later in her normal person. Especially that dratted game of golf, she added.

Betty had wonderful command of her body—as witness that stunt of standing on her head for long periods—but golf always exasperated her.

She brought back from the links an excellent definition—"You know, I can play this game a great deal better than I am—but I never do! " Now, in her flounderings in search of the smooth application to actual life of her inner attainments, she was puzzled. Finally the Invisibles threw her a line.

"You are forgetting to work in the nature of the substance," said they.

# 2.

The nature of the substance—here was a new phrase to add to the many catchwords the Invisibles had presented us. The inference was fairly clear, but what exactly did they mean? If a chemist wants to dissolve gold, he doesn't try to do it with sulphuric acid, does he?—I must condense and epitomize.—He knows better.

It is not gold's nature to respond to sulphuric acid. If an artist wants to express pure form, he does it in clay or marble or wood, he doesn't use paint. If he wants to express color and atmosphere and that sort of thing he uses a canvas; he does not daub up a statue, even if the Greeks did do it, or paste false whiskers on a portrait. Not if he is a good artist. And what would you think of a mechanic who built a machine out of wood instead of metal? Or a schoolmaster who tried to talk calculus to the kindergarten? Now, the Invisibles advised Betty, extend that to what you are trying to do—I am still condensing a mass of record. What are you working on? The world-people, individuals. You are trying to give them something, of yourself, aren't you? The trouble is that you are trying to give them all the same thing in the same way. You don't expect the same thing from each of them, do you? We do not want or find the same things in different people. What do you want of your friends, they finally challenged.

"Why," reflected Betty, "in some I want the warmth of uncritical affection, unquestioned acceptance in spite of surface imperfections. In others I want the light touch of humor and good fellowship playing lambent over our companionship. Still others help me to touch my highest point of mind and soul reaches." "And each of them wants something different from you," supplemented the Invisibles. "The art of living is to find out what you have for each other. A really skilled worker cherishes the character of the materials he works with, even to the point of utilizing a knot hole for decoration. He works in the nature of the substance." And, they added, it is rather naive to expect smooth sailing and cordial acceptance always.

"If you generate a force, it must meet opposition." Betty was beginning to see the point. "That's what I'm working on today. I go at it with a certain interest and appetite in trying it out; a humorous acceptance of a challenge with myself." That opposition, said the Invisibles, is itself a substance, with a nature of its own, that must be worked in.

"The first thing you must learn," they added, "is to accept opposition so in its entirety, so completely, that not one speck of attention is ever wasted on it, except for the intellectual appraisement of its strength and the planning for control of its effect." "I see," said Betty, "you do not say, 'Isn't it hateful I've got this? Isn't it disgusting that this happened!' You know that, if someone goes at you to overwhelm you with something, it is stupid to waste time and strength in reacting to it with resentment. You at once act together all your vigor to create exactly the opposite. . .

"The best course," elaborated the Invisibles, "is always to reduce your aims to their essentials, and then seek the cooperation of your material, however imperfect. Nor will you find this too difficult to accomplish—provided you keep as your chief aim the determination to proceed with the least friction and the most skill and sympathy, in the sense of an artist's sympathy with his work and material." "I needed that." Betty was appreciative. "You see, for a moment I was a little sad and puzzled about the uselessness of trying to bring a bit of real spirituality into ordinary life. The exquisite amount of devotion required to accomplish it, the creation of all the heart energy and absorption in it, in order to make it live in the atmosphere of everyday life—it's all so intangible to do, and people's reactions to it are so curious! It is like leading them into a refrigerating room or a furnace room—something that has an immediate reaction on them. You can't tell how they are going to take it." "Now the method we suggest in working in the nature of the substance," said the Invisibles, "is not to try immediately to graft on it what you have to bring. You should leave that to the constructive purpose with which you have unified yourself. Your part is to cultivate, in full enjoyment, the pitch which made that unification possible; and to try to lift from drabness and traditional isolations the

HUMAN nature." "It's a sort of idea of little shadings of ability to pick up from the human scrap heap and sense the bits of quality there. I find it a little hard—let it go," said Betty.

"My first translation of my experience," Betty tried to retrace the steps that had led her to this point, "was that I was not to reach restlessly and objectively hither and thither, but was to sit at home in myself and sense that self to the depth of my capacity of heart intelligence and comprehension. But that was not adequate: It is too limited.

"My next reaction to it was that through persistent practice I had become used to thinking of myself as vigorously centered in a point of power, capable of action on inferior substance. And that inferior substance is inferior because it has no free will to refuse my vigorous action, any more than metal can refuse to accept warmth when placed near the fire.

"But that was inadequate, too. Both those concepts were too limited to convey the scope of spiritual action. They are still molded by brain limitations; and yet both have necessary steps of truth embodied in them. The thing they lack is the universality of spiritual consciousness." "The only real way to work in the nature of the substance," contributed the Invisibles, "is through a generous and spontaneous blending with other lives in the universality common to all.

"it is very hard to drag forth the enduring element in each—the PERPETUAL person—, to throw calmly into the discard the barnacle parasite part," said the Invisibles.

"To work in the nature of the substance! " they exclaimed. "Why, if the world were only wise enough to do that, there would be little else to do. It is tolerance. It is the nth degree of humanitarianism. It is respect for the integrity of each individual soul. Those who have gained the habitual spiritual consciousness always work that way, in the nature of the substance; and it is in that way you can recognize them. In fact, working in the nature of the substance is the only way people can live together in peace."

# CHAPTER 21

# KINSHIP

## 1.

Of course, the Invisibles had told Betty all along, she was going to meet obstructions, throughout life. There is a necessary resistance, they indicated. How else can one rise? How else does an airplane rise, save through the resistance of the air? "After all," said they, "the time to practise anything enduring is in the times of stress...

And, they added dryly she would find no dearth of stress points. That is life; and life, in last analysis, is PEOPLE, just people. All the rest—the material comforts, the material securities, the material necessities—are met by the ingenuities of the mind and the energies of the body, and what they assure is bare existence. But it is in one's dealings with people, one's relations with people, one's gifts to and from people, that one meets the deeper resistance by which one's consciousness may rise. That is life; and that is the nature of its substance.

I think they were warning Betty not to expect everything to be all sweetness and light and brotherhood of man merely because she had come to understand the nature of her substance. Or perhaps not. They must have known Betty pretty well by now, and have been quite aware of her personal history. Without going into details, she had been enmeshed from childhood with a singularly complete array of self-centered and exacting neurasthenics, encroaching and demanding personalities with whom she had to cope; nor did her marriage free her from them entirely. The Invisibles classed them as "unreceptives," which seemed to me a masterpiece of understatement. If I had been consulted, I should have said that Betty needed no instruction on how to get along with people, prickly or otherwise. It is a literal fact that in the thirty-six years of our life together I never knew her to quarrel, with anybody; not even with me! I am certain this is no fatuous reconstruction because, occasionally for the fun of it, I would try to prod her into a fight, and never succeeded. Oh, she could be firm enough, as many—again including myself—found out, but in some mysterious and Betty's fashion she managed it without battle or indignation.

Be that as it may, the Invisibles and Betty embarked on a statement of principles concerning conflict.

## 2.

"First of all," the Invisibles began, apropos of "unreceptive" people, "you must protect yourself from getting in their zone of action. You must first insulate yourself. Insulation is not unsympathetic! It is just the precaution the doctor takes against infection. So insulation is not isolation.

"Next," they advised, "keep yourself whole. The strategy of war is to divide the enemy. Recognize instantly when you are being divided. Laugh a good strong laugh, and rush forward. At the moment of unity surge onward in spite of obstructions. Whenever provoking things happen, look on yourself as in danger of being the vanquished instead of the victor, the captured instead of the captor. Each time you score, it is a definite count; it is not erased. It is like acquiring something; makes what you are doing easier. It is a great help each time you hold fast and don't get captured.

"Do not start out expecting to be flattered by spectacular results. Just plan to keep going for the satisfaction of occupying your place in the greater scheme. There will always be moments of full realization, the blooming and fruition natural to all life. That also will come to you in its turn. It is not all strain and effort.

"Do not," they continued, "be discouraged even when failure turns into something like actual defeat. This is FUN, you know, like gardening or healing or painting a picture or any other creative satisfaction.

You decide, as a master should, how things should be, and you make them so.

You dominate your materials, instead of being dominated; and because of your strength of perception you are able to look beyond inevitable failure to inevitable success, Pay no attention to defeat. When you look at the defeat side it is like compound interest. The next time you will have to overcome this time, and the failure that went before, and the one before that...

"And finally," they completed their fist, "watch your fore—determinations. Bad days must not be bad before they begin. Put your consciousness on the higher level, before you start out every day.

You need more preparedness for yourself. That is your job.

PARTICULARIZED foredetermination," they discriminated, "not just hazy.

Work it over carefully, as you would an architect's blueprint. That is vitalized thinking. It's different, a creative thinking. There's substance to it. It is really a higher form of thought." "I do try to work it," said Betty. "I know the law, but—oh dear, it's so unpopular! Everybody thinks it's mushy. They don't know what I'm doing." "These points are the important ones," summed up the Invisibles, "the robustness of your intent, and the temporary quality of seeming defeat.

Remember we are concerning ourselves with the laws of a higher force which must, eventually, overcome things potent only in their own generation and time." "All right," agreed Betty. "Every time I feel annoyed or deflected or crossed, I'll think of myself as in danger of capture by inferior force.

Instead of cutting myself off from my reinforcements, I'll try to utilize them in commonplace moments like that, and not keep them for big, noble occasions." "In your relations to people," said the Invisibles, "it isn't at all this everything-to-everybody, hand-grasp idea. That's the cheap imitation; very cheap! There is dignity and reserve and depth to the real thing. It is just a QUIET feeling, a silent feeling of kinship and sympathetic response, instead of the usual indifference."

# 3.

KINSHIP proved to be a key word.

"U, S, us; N, E, double S, ness: Us-ness," the Invisibles started Betty off, one day.

"There is no such word," she commented, "but that is what they say. . .

Anyhow, I can't separate myself into a hard-shelled detached unit any more.

"Apparently I'm made up of fundamentals which every created thing shares to a greater or lesser degree. Therefore I'm sympathetically connected with, and share in the life of, everything through the ingredients we have in common. That, very vaguely, is the Us-ness of it... I can't say it very well; but it's a very nice feeling." "Don't look at this too closely," advised the Invisibles, "don't analyze it. Take it as a broad general feeling until it grows and forms." "I am in a wonderful atmosphere," said Betty. "It is teeming with life, and it is plastic somehow. I feel people all around me, acting chemically on each other—just like chemical action, only it is spiritual. We laugh at the idea of auras, but they are quite real in a way. You go near a fire, and that has an aura; so has ice. Only with people it seems quite a tangible thing. It extends just a certain radius around. When people approach within that radius their auras intermingle, and at once chemical action begins." She was silent so long I finally asked what she was doing.

"I am keeping quiet," she replied, "just to see what belongs to us all in common. It is a strange companionship. When I separate myself and enter each one of you, it is the jolliest kind of companionship. None of the little superficial differences matters at all. It is very funny: I like to laugh, and yet it would sound inane were I to tell you that just laughing, for itself done, Without any specified joke, is a nice kind of intermingling.

It's a good deal like having lots of relatives," Betty continued after a pause. "That's the heavy side of it! But the nice side of it is that you can go around feeling relationship with all the beautiful things in the world. You can call out to each other. That's much better than being a stranger in the world, isn't it—this claim of kinship to all created things.

"I can go around and call to things, call to a nice cloud I see up there: 'Hello there! We're related to each other on such and such a side.' Or I can say to my big tree and all the little birds under it in the nest, 'I claim a bit of you all.' Wind and sun; they're touching and quickening the bit of me that is wind and sun. It's so much nicer to let them all enter in, and welcome them, and exchange courtesies with them, than to be so hard-shelled and alone...

"I'm so anxious to keep going around and seeing how much of things claim me, finding out which are my near relatives and which my far ones.

They're all different. There are the stars: they are pretty distantly related. I can't do more than respect and admire them...

"I can't tell you how it changes things to think this way. The sympathetic contact makes it possible to contain the whole world within yourself, expanding to contain them all. I'm astonished at the feel of it. And it's such fun! All the infinite variations are such FUN—mixing up all the shades and colors and infinite variations! I'm having a LOVELY time! Please let me enjoy it...

"It's such a new world I've discovered. I wonder why I didn't always know it. I've always WANTED to feel that way. I want to whistle with the wind! I want to swish with the tides! I want to lullaby with the moon! I want to be loud with the thunder! I want to cr-e-e-p into small places, and I want to soar into big ones! I'm all tingling and glowing with the warmth of the sun. I think I will go now where the cold lives." She stopped short, struck with a new and splendid idea.

"I wonder," she speculated doubtfully, "if I could be an earthquake." The thought of Betty as an earthquake was too much for me; I shouted aloud. She joined my laughter, but half-heartedly.

"I'd have to work my way up to that," she conceded.

She waved her extended hand, now here, now there.

"Anyway, it's like waving to somebody, or letting him go by with no recognition at all. I want to go around just greeting things! "The simplest expression I can reduce it to is in the word reciprocity," she decided. "That makes an actual thing, like an electric current. I must have very simple things like that, so they will stay in my everyday mind."

# 4.

"I am," said Betty in her next approach, "face to face with this vast level of consciousness that is back of human consciousness. They show me a great rope twisted of many strands... I don't understand it. It runs through us all... It is the connecting link. It is the connection through which we act on each other on this level. When we touch it, it is charged with life and vitality, an open way of wisdom and understanding. If you touched, reached this level, somebody would answer somewhere if you had a real need they could supply. It is the universal conductor in some way.

"Never mind how simplified your consciousness may become," the Invisibles told her, "nor how clear your aim or your comprehension of what you are after, nor how devoutly you may follow it, it does not work unless you have sympathetic comprehension of the interelation." "I am almost afraid to try to put the relationship into words," said Betty, "and yet I must struggle with it." She attacked the problem of expression from many angles. "The great ocean connecting all islands and continents—all the parceled—off objective things, of however great magnitude, are but the islands and continents among and around which flows the great carrier," was one effort. But that did not work; for, said she, the universal relationship not only flows around, but through.

It is the common substance of all creation, and it is in that common substance that created things meet and act on one another in proper process, intermingle in their common denominator, so to speak, and yet— "I've made an awful mess of trying to tell you!" Betty gave up in despair. "I won't talk any more. I've said it badly because I gave the impression of a merging of INDIVIDUALITIES. It is not that. They ARE distinct; but it's the merging of the substance possessed by all of them, which, kept uppermost, produces the magic." "This is very advanced teaching," warned the Invisibles. "We are not sure that it is wise to precipitate it, but we'll sketch its meaning.

Very briefly and crudely, it is to this effect: "The undeveloped being lives in isolation of consciousness within himself, his village, his town, his country depending on how far along he is, always contained within definite personality limits, separated from other creations by the confines of his senses and sympathies. The developed man is as different a creature in the breadth of his perceptions as is a walnut in its difference from the winds. The developed man can search out any distance with an extension of himself, his full consciousness concentrated at any point he desires. He assumes kinship with other consciousnesses as poignantly as with his own." "It is just like the radio," contributed Betty. "You pick out the right wave length and travel on it." "This sympathetic assumption of kinship," continued the Invisibles, "empowers him with the attributes of the higher consciousness. And one result of this is that he is no longer, while living as other men, restricted by their limitations of position—position in the geometrical sense—because anything he turns his attention to ardently, anything he loves, he BECOMES, in this greater entity. This greater entity gives him the ability to broadcast himself, to travel to it sympathetically, as it were, on its individual wave length." "It may not sound like much at first," said Betty, "but think of the stupendous power of this faculty when one actually grows into full possession of it. One no longer occupies a one-pointed position. One's heart extensions are potentially universal...

"Sometimes," said she, groping for it, "I believe that just shutting your eyes and loving people is the real way. If I kept them open, I'd be so busy looking at the outsides of you. And now I don't have to: I can just shut my eyes and love you as you register on me—I can't say it very well—not what you get snarled up trying to DO, but what you have inside of you that you want to BE.—I must remember that's the way to do with people.

"Don't have to keep your eyes shut all the time; just now and then,—but it's easier to keep on loving them when you do!" The Invisibles approved this.

"You can ignore the misrepresenting agents of the man—his habits, indulgences, dormancies and insist on dealing with his possibilities," said they.

"You see," Betty repeated a standard complaint, "I was sad and puzzled again about the uselessness of trying to bring real spirituality into ordinary life. It's so apt to make you shirk your devotion to other more obvious things. I was so puzzled about it. I understood my bit of power.

I'd learned a little bit about my own heart, and had timidly but unashamed, let a few other people feel it—given it to them whether they wanted to stamp on it or not. People's reactions are so very curious. Do they want to acclimatize themselves, or do they want to stay as they are?

# 5.

"The greater entity," or, as the Invisibles put it at times, Kinship, is the wave length to which one tunes in order to really communicate with fellow beings. And with that came, to us both, a great illumination.

For the most part the aim of Betty's first training had seemed to be the fitting her for easy communication with the Invisibles. Now we perceived that all of it, the earlier and the later, had been TO FIT HER FOR REAL COMMUNICATION WITH HER FELLOW-BEINGS WHEREVER THEY MIGHT BE! And the method she had learned is the method of communication everywhere.

Exactly so the Invisibles communicated with her.

So now they told us a little of how they did it.

"In approaching a person with whom we wish to communicate," said they, "our preliminary preparation is the holding off from that person, temporarily, the pressure of conditions relative to his normal life. We lift the weight. After that pressure is lifted, it is like looking into a lighted room from the outside dark; or peering into the different element of an aquarium. That is the first process.

"Perhaps," they continued, "you will understand this better if you think of it as just like any of your other closer contacts. Take friendship, for example: you approach your real friends with exactly the same process of lightening pressures, of warmth in each other's atmospheres, of getting directly in touch with the intimate sides of them which are less recognized by the world in general.

"What have we now? We have a human being momentarily surrounded by an atmosphere of higher potentiality. The process that follows is to observe his reactions to it; the type of thing presenting itself immediately to his consciousness. The drift of this native tendency regulates to a certain degree the material possible to impart to him.

The next process is one of inhibiting undesirables, relapses to habitual methods of thought.

"In other words, we select from his native equipment, when freshly released, the thing most suitable to our purposes. The skill on our side is in the correspondence possible between what we desire to impart and what the subject under observation has avidity enough to take. That avidity is an essential ingredient in common. He may not in normal consciousness be aware of this avidity. It may be a totally buried part of his spiritually arrested nature. If however it exists at all, it can under skillful treatment be called out, educated up to our own purposes." Here again was working in the nature of the substance.

But Betty was back with her more immediate job. She interrupted to call it "the utilizing of kinship, the connective mind, in the world of affairs." "I'm connected with everything by one of my ingredients," she declared.

"I don't understand this... I'm just trying to grasp the feel of it.

. . . That is what I am coming into now."

# CHAPTER 22

# RADIATION

## 1.

Recorded sessions of formal instruction, as such, practically ceased with 1934. This ended fifteen years of rigorous schooling. Apparently Betty's "outfit for eternity," as she had once called it, was complete.

She had come into possessions, and she had gained conscious use of them.

That use appeared to boil down to the ability to COMMUNICATE with her fellow beings, visible or invisible, here in our obstructed aspect of the universe, or elsewhere in the unobstructed.

One thing more, however, remained to be brought to the forefront of her consciousness; and that one thing was in the line of attainment rather than of instruction. Betty had not only LEARNED something, she had BECOME something. And what she had become possessed its own power of action, by the very nature of its own substance. This was the last concept Betty must get clear for me and her own conscious understanding.

## 2.

"They are showing me," she began her description, "a very advanced method of reaching us. A special kind of adjustment is involved: the sort of thing, the specialists over here use when they look at us. It shows our world very dark-black. Here and there are spots of glow or phosphorescence from the more developed among us...

Now I am taking the point of view of a very highly developed person on this side, one of the really great Radiant Ones. If I were such a one, and wanted to help somebody who showed this phosphorescent glow in the darkness, how would I go about it? Why, I think I would just come close and contemplate him, and so bring the effect of my RADIATION on him. And what would be the result of that? "First of all, it would burn away or melt away the external dull crust, exposing the core of his reality. And that core would then reflect back.

It would not glow of itself, but it could now reflect the light of my radiation, and thus becoming visible to the man—make him visible to himself.

"Do you see? It was all dark to him before, but now he can see himself because of this reflected light, and can perceive his needs and lacks and all that. And then while the glow is on him, and only then, he can write to himself about it, or talk to himself about it, in detail—just what he needs. But all I have done is to bring my radiation to him."

## 3.

How was she to make the application to creative living? She went deep into an experimental silence.

"You remember," she was ready to report to me at last, "that intensifying of your out-going impulses? Well, the exercise I've been doing is like that, only it is no longer in a straight-line channel, as it were. I am getting the circular action of it, like a lawn sprinkler.

I keep turning it, almost like a searchlight; the beam is like a searchlight ray, only it's all warm and human and happy natural enthusiasm and interest, as when one approaches one's hobbles, affections or loves. I am exercising myself by turning a complete circle with it. At each point it touches I see with new and sympathetic eyes right into the soul of the thing, and my kinship and responsibilities with it...

And after a long silence: "I don't actually have to turn myself now; I can do it in almost any direction...

"Now they've taken it away. It was to give greater flexibility to the idea of propulsion... RADIATION is better. That was an actual practice in radiation...

"There's something more about it; but I've got to go deeper to get it...

"How do I do it?" she pondered. "It sounds silly to say 'think horizontally,' doesn't it? But that is it. It is as though the spiritual force were fluid, and by thinking horizontally it could be made to flow in all directions about you, reaching others and bringing others to you in a single all-embracing exchange of vitality." Ensued another of the long pauses that always indicated work was going on in which I had no present concern. But it must have been productive work, for Betty resumed almost breathlessly: I am gaining strength," she told me, "almost beyond my ability to contain... I lead a dance, I fling, I spread warmth, I rush on, incandescent with life! Just let me travel on in this glowing way for a while.

An interval followed.

"I am going through a change," Betty explained at last, "a curious radiating, convexing and pouring out from myself, as definite as though I'd been turned inside out...

"Why! When you're arranged in that old CONCAVE shape, you present no surface of participation in life! You are an alien shape, just a dormant seed—encasement of life! I don't want to be that way again, ever, just concavely containing my little bit. It is all right, but it is ungerminated." Another pause.

"Take something exhilarating," Betty continued, "take a salt-sea-washed body and the cool sweet union of it with the great fresh element. Keep going out, out, out beyond the mere exhilaration. You have turned the other way, curving out, a radiation of yourself—radiation...

Betty's enthusiasm became breathless.

"No words exist which can exactly express or convey this inner flame," the Invisibles encouraged her. "It is one of the most silently apparent of possessions. It makes its way without words or exhibition. It travels from heart to heart in its own channels of expression and exchange. And you always sense it, even if you do not acknowledge it with anything better than mental sophistication, as toward something simple folk and peasants have. For it is a unique and unmistakable thing, this rare, luminous, stimulating, kindly radiation of one who conducts, even though unconsciously, the current of universal force." Her elation ebbed.

"I don't quite understand that—too big for me. I have the feeling of it: I know what it feels like to manifest in various forms of life. But I can work only in the emotional desire of it." The Invisibles warned her against fostering the idea of an ebb. This radiation, it seemed, was the one thing that did not work in alternate rhythm of activity and rest.

"Remember this well," said they, "radiance should not wax and wane in power depending on the earth's recognition of it. It is the private affair of a surface, continually existent under all conditions, whether or not someone sees the sun shining on it. It is his own self-of-self, his own bit of frequency that he alone can manipulate. Therein only is happiness secure. The control of destiny is in a steady maintenance of a course satisfactory to your highest apex of perception. Radiance is the reward of this permanence of heart." "Pretty soon," said Betty, "I'll start out and radiate more strongly, pulse myself along. I feel like a baby that must wonder how people move around so fast and surely. I wonder how they dare do it. Radiation increases my surface." She added, "You are tremendously responsible for your radius. That is what we are judged by." "Each person's deeds," said the Invisibles, "float, as it were, in a certain atmosphere created by himself. This fostering atmosphere is not sufficiently understood.

"We recognize and acknowledge things almost as intangible, such as the chemical effect of the sun's ray's on plants, the warmth and other conditions indispensable to growth. The plant survives or perishes according as the climate is suitable to its needs and character. The warmth of the human heart associated with directing power, discriminating intelligence—it is variously named—makes this humanly fostering climate. It is not understood as a parallel to the climatic condition with plants. It must be. As soon as it is so understood, it is going to fall in the category of things cultivated as essential to life." "This atmosphere we radiate—" contributed Betty,—"I don't know how else to say it—I see in it the potency of the Djinn to the bottle—a Djinn which is released by expansion of the heart. The moment you take the trouble to acquaint yourself with your own heart, to exercise it and extend its perceptions, then you've begun to release your powerful Djinn-radiation. I luxuriate in it; but this luxuriating is the sort that goes out and can be picked up by others. It is not a selfly thing.—There is a difference: selfish is stern and haughty; selfly is merely limited...

"It is fun to be alive enough to throw out sparks this way," she cried enthusiastically. "Some people are sufficiently inflammable to get the spark: on others it just sizzles and goes out because of the sogginess of them... I wish I could describe what I'm doing...

She broke her exultation with a sudden complaint.

"Sometimes when I am happy, working this way in heart substances, head substances keep getting in the way, analyzing me as an introspective fool." She paused, then went on with confidence. "But I know they are wrong. I see their inferiority and limitations in span. They are all right—for their job. But the heart substances are more powerful, more enduring." "The thing is so fundamental," the Invisible endorsed this, "that its reality can only be FELT, and not contained in written words. It is akin to light and heat and energy, which ARE first and manifest second. The interest with which one pursues a pet hobby comes nearer to the radiation idea than any other, magnetically attracting to you everything along the line, giving and receiving with case and pleasure. Love, humor, interested creation of the kind one does pleasurably in one's avocations—every unobstructed channel of daily life endowed with ease and richness of output: all these are akin." But Betty had passed her momentary depression.

"I feel so powerful!" she cried. "I'm so powerful and sure, so ABSORB-ING of everything around me. And yet I'm not just a fungus-growth absorbing.

I'm occupying more life: that's what I'm doing! That's a nice idea, but I can't help thinking how funny it is for me—I'm so piffling!" "Radiation is penetrative to a degree unknown to denser matter," stated the Invisibles further, extending Betty's lawn sprinkler concept.

"Roughly speaking, for visualization purposes, its action is not confined to a direct line, but is also encircling. In other words, when this force is sent out forward to an object, it is also received abeam and astern, above and below.

"And as it is extraordinarily penetrative and encircling, so it is also, paradoxically, extremely personal; more so than any earthly possession, for its very existence depends upon yourself—your inner, not your nervously controlled self. It is the most individualistic possession imaginable, as well as the most universal.

"GERMINATED spirituality is radioactive," they added. "That is what makes the difference between the cultivation and expansion of it, and when it is merely potentially or rather dormant motivating in you. It is what gauges personality, the radius of a human being's life influence.

"Think about this happily, without effort of any kind. Strain will never accomplish anything but defeat. If radiation were anything but illumination in rapture, it would not be radiation."

# 4.

"Listen!" breathed Betty.

Down in the canon, outside our window, a wood thrush was singing, repeating over and over again his liquid musical phrases.

"That is what I mean!" she cried. "That bird! His very best—but plus his response." She puzzled a long time over some instruction or explanation that was obviously being conveyed to her. "Oh, I see!" she exclaimed at last—the thrush was continuing to sing—"He is still doing it because he isn't filled up yet. You see, he fills up magnetically, by giving out.

That is the way creatures get their life force,—the frog croaks, and gets his that way. People get some when they laugh or sing together." She contemplated this for some time.

"I used to think I was reaching toward some distant and occult sort of sense," she ventured. "Now I find I'm just making thinner and thinner my walls in order to blend myself with forces right at hand; forces that all the plants and beasts possess." "Until there is worship in the heart," this from the Invisibles, "a development of intense perception of something vastly superior to the sovereignty of the brain, until there is the recognition of your sun—until that is activating, all else is but an intellectual concept.

Unless that warmth is within you, a living flame ever ready for action, it will be better for you to wait without the gate." "Before I start anything," promised Betty, "I'll drop my consciousness into place as a link between the purpose I do not understand and the little act of which I am master. It is the consciousness of the hook-up and the practice of it that makes it work, lets in the power. It is just a workaday, natural action—my two hands directed by my spirit. I'll just say to the unknown Purpose, 'I am ready when you are,' and keep a steady confidence in the purpose at hand, and it will grow in ripeness better than I could plan." A silence.

"We are making a great road over which a noble traveler approaches," said Betty.

## THE END

# Paperbacks also available from
# White Crow Books

Elsa Barker—*Letters from a Living Dead Man*
ISBN 978-1-907355-83-7

Elsa Barker—*War Letters from the Living Dead Man*
ISBN 978-1-907355-85-1

Elsa Barker—*Last Letters from the Living Dead Man*
ISBN 978-1-907355-87-5

Richard Maurice Bucke—*Cosmic Consciousness*
ISBN 978-1-907355-10-3

Arthur Conan Doyle—*The Edge of the Unknown*
ISBN 978-1-907355-14-1

Arthur Conan Doyle—*The New Revelation*
ISBN 978-1-907355-12-7

Arthur Conan Doyle—*The Vital Message*
ISBN 978-1-907355-13-4

Arthur Conan Doyle with Simon Parke—*Conversations with Arthur Conan Doyle*
ISBN 978-1-907355-80-6

Meister Eckhart with Simon Parke—*Conversations with Meister Eckhart*
ISBN 978-1-907355-18-9

D. D. Home—*Incidents in my Life Part 1*
ISBN 978-1-907355-15-8

Mme. Dunglas Home; edited, with an Introduction, by Sir Arthur Conan Doyle—*D. D. Home: His Life and Mission*
ISBN 978-1-907355-16-5

Edward C. Randall—*Frontiers of the Afterlife*
ISBN 978-1-907355-30-1

Rebecca Ruter Springer—*Intra Muros: My Dream of Heaven*
ISBN 978-1-907355-11-0

Leo Tolstoy, edited by Simon Parke—*Forbidden Words*
ISBN 978-1-907355-00-4

Leo Tolstoy—*A Confession*
ISBN 978-1-907355-24-0

Leo Tolstoy—*The Gospel in Brief*
ISBN 978-1-907355-22-6

Leo Tolstoy—*The Kingdom of God is Within You*
ISBN 978-1-907355-27-1

Leo Tolstoy—*My Religion: What I Believe*
ISBN 978-1-907355-23-3

Leo Tolstoy—*On Life*
ISBN 978-1-907355-91-2

Leo Tolstoy—*Twenty-three Tales*
ISBN 978-1-907355-29-5

Leo Tolstoy—*What is Religion and other writings*
ISBN 978-1-907355-28-8

Leo Tolstoy—*Work While Ye Have the Light*
ISBN 978-1-907355-26-4

Leo Tolstoy—*The Death of Ivan Ilyich*
ISBN 978-1-907661-10-5

Leo Tolstoy—*Resurrection*
ISBN 978-1-907661-09-9

Leo Tolstoy with Simon Parke—*Conversations with Tolstoy*
ISBN 978-1-907355-25-7

Howard Williams with an Introduction by Leo Tolstoy—*The Ethics of Diet: An Anthology of Vegetarian Thought*
ISBN 978-1-907355-21-9

Vincent Van Gogh with Simon Parke—*Conversations with Van Gogh*
ISBN 978-1-907355-95-0

Wolfgang Amadeus Mozart with Simon Parke—*Conversations with Mozart*
ISBN 978-1-907661-38-9

Jesus of Nazareth with Simon Parke—
*Conversations with Jesus of Nazareth*
ISBN 978-1-907661-41-9

Thomas à Kempis with Simon
Parke—*The Imitation of Christ*
ISBN 978-1-907661-58-7

Julian of Norwich with Simon
Parke—*Revelations of Divine Love*
ISBN 978-1-907661-88-4

Allan Kardec—*The Spirits Book*
ISBN 978-1-907355-98-1

Allan Kardec—*The Book on Mediums*
ISBN 978-1-907661-75-4

Emanuel Swedenborg—*Heaven and Hell*
ISBN 978-1-907661-55-6

P.D. Ouspensky—*Tertium Organum:
The Third Canon of Thought*
ISBN 978-1-907661-47-1

Dwight Goddard—*A Buddhist Bible*
ISBN 978-1-907661-44-0

Michael Tymn—*The Afterlife Revealed*
ISBN 978-1-970661-90-7

Michael Tymn—*Transcending the
Titanic: Beyond Death's Door*
ISBN 978-1-908733-02-3

Guy L. Playfair—*If This Be Magic*
ISBN 978-1-907661-84-6

Guy L. Playfair—*The Flying Cow*
ISBN 978-1-907661-94-5

Guy L. Playfair —*This House is Haunted*
ISBN 978-1-907661-78-5

Carl Wickland, M.D.—
*Thirty Years Among the Dead*
ISBN 978-1-907661-72-3

John E. Mack—*Passport to the Cosmos*
ISBN 978-1-907661-81-5

Peter & Elizabeth Fenwick—
*The Truth in the Light*
ISBN 978-1-908733-08-5

Erlendur Haraldsson—
*Modern Miracles*
ISBN 978-1-908733-25-2

Erlendur Haraldsson—
*At the Hour of Death*
ISBN 978-1-908733-27-6

Erlendur Haraldsson—
*The Departed Among the Living*
ISBN 978-1-908733-29-0

Brian Inglis—*Science and Parascience*
ISBN 978-1-908733-18-4

Brian Inglis—*Natural and Supernatural:
A History of the Paranormal*
ISBN 978-1-908733-20-7

Ernest Holmes—*The Science of Mind*
ISBN 978-1-908733-10-8

Victor & Wendy Zammit —*A Lawyer
Presents the Evidence For the Afterlife*
ISBN 978-1-908733-22-1

Casper S. Yost—*Patience
Worth: A Psychic Mystery*
ISBN 978-1-908733-06-1

William Usborne Moore—
*Glimpses of the Next State*
ISBN 978-1-907661-01-3

William Usborne Moore—
*The Voices*
ISBN 978-1-908733-04-7

John W. White—
*The Highest State of Consciousness*
ISBN 978-1-908733-31-3

Stafford Betty—
*The Imprisoned Splendor*
ISBN 978-1-907661-98-3

Paul Pearsall, Ph.D. —
*Super Joy*
ISBN 978-1-908733-16-0

**All titles available as eBooks, and selected titles available in Hardback and Audiobook formats from www.whitecrowbooks.com**

www.ingramcontent.com/pod-product-compliance
Lightning Source LLC
Chambersburg PA
CBHW020912180626
46816CB00007BA/2368